OUTLAWS

Volume 11

True Tales of the Old West

by

Charles L. Convis

PIONEER PRESS, CARSON CITY, NEVADA

Library of Congress Catalog Card Number: 96-68502

ISBN 1-892156-01-6 (Volume)
ISBN 0-9651954-0-6 (Series)

Printed by
KNI, Incorporated
Anaheim, California

CONTENTS

ILLUSTRATIONS

2

MUCHO HOMBRE

Juan Cortina was either an outlaw or a patriot, depending on your point of view. He was a juvenile killer. Later he led a thousand-man army to whip the combined forces of two nations. He stole almost a million horses and cows. Governor of his state, he almost became his nation's president.

Juan resembled his mother's people with his light skin, blue eyes, sandy hair, and outwardly gentle manners. Those ancestors settled north of the Rio Grande in 1767 with a royal grant from the King of Spain. But Juan got his ferocity, rebellious spirit, and physical endurance from his Indian father.

Juan's widowed mother raised him on the family ranch, Rancho Santa Rita, seven miles north of Brownsville. Although more Texian than Mexican, Juan fought with the Mexicans in their war against the United States. He could neither read nor write, but he became a great leader of men.

One of the disputes in the war was the sovereignty of the 150-mile strip between the Nueces River and the Rio Grande. Neither country governed the area, and desperadoes from both nations hid out there to loot and steal.

Cortina most hated Charles Stillman. He had come from New England to be a Matamoros merchant. He sold arms to Mexican rebels. Cortina, a Mexican citizen, despised him.

Young Cortina killed several men while protecting his family's ranch from thieves. Stillman, by then the founder and boss of Brownsville on the United States side of the river, got grand jury indictments. But no one would arrest Cortina.

Other resentful young Mexicans joined Cortina's band, and the frightened citizens of Brownsville hired a town marshal to protect them. Marshal Bob Shears' first instructions were to bring in Juan Cortina.

When Cortina and a few followers came to Brownsville on July 13, 1859, Shears got the drop on one of them in a saloon. Cortina crashed his horse through the batwing doors, shot Shears down, scooped up his man, and carried him out. A thirty-man posse chased the band to Rancho Santa Rita and met a hail of bullets.

Instead of arresting Cortina, they took back his demand that several persons be turned over to him to deal with in his own way. The list included Stillman, along with Mifflin Kenedy and Richard King, owners of the giant King Ranch. These three had contributed the money to hire the marshal.

Cortina's band grew with the addition of more outlaws, both Mexican and American, some genuine Mexican patriots, and a few adventurers with loyalty to no country. Cortina captured Fort Brown from the United States Cavalry and sacked Brownsville. The beleaguered Americans pleaded for help from the Mexican military in Matamoros. General Carvajal, a hard-boiled relative of Cortina, marched his troops across the border. But Cortina withdrew to avoid a confrontation. His band stole horses and cattle, interrupted mail and steamer traffic, and isolated Brownsville from the rest of the world.

A scout slipped past Cortina's patrols to reach Laredo, two hundred miles away. Messengers rode to Corpus Christi, San Antonio, and San Patricio, pleading for help. Relief parties of Texas Rangers headed south. General Carvajal took command of a combined force of Mexican and American soldiers. They fought Cortina at Palo Alto. Cortina's band killed twenty, with only a few casualties of their own.

Then Colonel Robert E. Lee, stationed in San Antonio, took command of all the forces. His orders, however, were canceled when he was sent to Harpers Ferry, West Virginia, where John Brown had just captured an arsenal.

Cortina's victory over Texas Rangers, volunteers, and United States and Mexican soldiers at Palo Alto was particularly sweet. He had fought on the losing side at the same place, thirteen years before.

In December a combined attacking force of three hundred surprised a Cortina lieutenant and routed his men with heavy casualties. Cortina retreated north, destroying the towns of Edinburg and Rio Grande City. But the Rangers defeated the band on Christmas Day, as the Cortinistos celebrated with too much mescal.

Cortina led his defeated remnant into Mexico. He reorganized his band, added volunteers, and, for many years, continued raiding into Texas. Cortina became mayor of Matamoros and Governor of Tamaulipas. He fought against the puppet ruler, Maximilian, and was beaten for the presidency of Mexico by his cousin, Porfirio Diaz.

Juan Cortina was *mucho hombre* in two nations.

Suggested reading, Ruel McDaniel, "Juan Cortina - Hero or Bandit?" in *The Best of True West* (New York: Julian Messner, 1964).

SCOURGE OF THE OUTLAWS

Joseph A. (Jack) Slade worked for Russell, Majors & Waddell when Ben Holladay bought the company in 1861. Holladay knew he would need a good crew to make the company profitable. Indians, road agents, and dishonest employees had put Russell's outfit out of business. Holladay hired the toughest men the Russell outfit had.

Ben Holladay was big and rough and made his own law. He wanted superintendents like himself. He had heard of Jack Slade and the time Jack tangled with another employee. Jack and the teamster had drawn their pistols at the same instant. Jack smiled and convinced his opponent that they should drop their weapons and fight bare fisted. The teamster tossed his weapon away. Jack laughed as he gunned the unarmed man down.

Holladay thought Slade was the best man he had, so he put him on the wildest division on the stageline — across northeastern Colorado from the Wyoming border to Julesburg. Slade made the border station his headquarters and named it Virginia Dale after his common-law wife.

A faithful employee, Slade sent road agents and horse thieves running. He kept his men in line, his roads in good condition, and his stations well stocked. He was as charming with customers as he was vicious with dishonest employees and bandits. A dead shot, no one knows how many men he killed, all for the sake of the company. Soon he was the most loyal and the most feared man on the payroll.

Slade had become a legend. When writer Samuel Clemens went to Nevada by stagecoach, he said the drivers talked only about three things: California gold, Nevada silver, and Jack Slade. Clemens interviewed Slade at a breakfast stop and wrote about him in *Roughing It.*

"The most gentlemanly-appearing, quiet and affable officer in the Overland Company's service sat at the head of the table, at my elbow. Right at my side was the actual ogre who, in fights and brawls and various ways, had taken the lives of twenty-six human beings. He was so friendly and so gentle-spoken that I warmed to him in spite of his awful luster. It was hardly possible to realize that this pleasant person was the pitiless scourge of the outlaws, the raw head and bloody bones the nursing mothers of the mountains terrified their children with."

But heavy drinking turned Slade into a beast who began

killing for meanness alone. At a bar in Green River, Wyoming, a drunk dared Slade to shoot him. Slade, drinking heavily himself, ignored the man at first. But when the helpless old drunk persisted, Slade shot him down.

Slade's cruel execution of Jules Reni, who had been robbing the company blind, was talked about all over the country. Gradually Slade turned from a company hatchet-man to an outlaw himself. Then he began robbing the company which he had served so devotedly. Road agents once again terrified the Julesburg Division, and the company suspected its superintendent was teaming up with them. But Holladay, remembering how Slade had cleaned up his worst division, was reluctant to act.

Then Slade destroyed the Sutler's store at Fort Halleck, Wyoming, and the fort commander told Holladay that Slade must go. Holladay rode to Virginia Dale. He did not look forward to firing Slade, but he was not afraid to do it.

Slade was drunk when Holladay found him.

"It's over, Slade," he bellowed. "Pick up your things and get out."

Slade's brutality increased after he was cut off from the company he had once served. He shot a man down at the man's home, dragged him into his house where his wife and three children huddled in fear, and set the house afire. The whole family perished.

Slade shot a bartender for commenting about the way Slade had executed Jules Reni. A woman holding a baby ran screaming from the saloon; Slade whirled and shot her down, too.

Although no one dared challenge Slade on his rampages, he and Virginia grew tired of being outcasts. They moved north to Virginia City, a lawless place in Montana Territory.

Slade started a ranch, and he also freighted supplies from Fort Benton to the mines. But every so often he would get drunk and terrorize Virginia City. In 1864, after an all night drinking bout, he tore up the furniture in his hotel room. The landlord appealed to the local vigilantes. They captured Slade, dragged him to a corral with a high pole over the gate, and hanged him.

Suggested reading: Ellis Lucia, *The Saga of Ben Holladay, Giant of the Old West* (New York: Hastings House, 1959).

TEEN AGE REVENGE

Joaquin Murieta was California's most famous outlaw in gold rush days. He was born in Mexico into a prominent Basque family. He had a fine education, and was a good dancer and a skillful guitar player.

In 1849, when he was seventeen, Murieta eloped with a sixteen-year-old neighbor girl, Rosita Feliz. The young couple stopped at a church in Hermosillo long enough to pledge their troth before the Virgin; they galloped on to California.

Murieta bought mining tools and supplies in San Francisco. Then he and Rosita rode east into the foothills along the Stanislaus River to stake their claim.

Murieta discovered a placer deposit of gold. He worked his claim, built a cabin, and looked forward to a bright future with his beautiful bride and a rich gold mine. But desperadoes jumped the claim one night, bound and beat Murieta, and raped Rosita.

When he recovered from his injuries, Murieta found work as a monte dealer in Murphy's Diggins, near where his half-brother, Jesus, lived. Rosita worked on a ranch near Mariposa. One night Joaquin borrowed his brother's horse to ride home. Twenty miners intercepted him, claiming the horse belonged to one of them. They rode with Joaquin back to his brother, but they refused to believe Jesus when he said he had bought the animal from a stranger. They hanged Jesus and flogged Joaquin.

After Joaquin buried his brother, he knelt beside the grave, his bowie knife raised aloft. With tears streaming down his face, he pledged to devote the rest of his life to killing Americans.

"May my soul never know peace," he whispered, "until my hands are dyed deep in the blood of my enemies."

Within a few weeks five bodies from the twenty-man mob who had hanged Jesus had been found. Each victim's throat bore a lariat burn, and each body was carved into pieces. The other fifteen miners fled. Eventually they were all killed, too.

Leaders of established bandit bands joined Murieta. His main lieutenants were five men who also took his first name. One other, Manuel Garcia, took the name Three Fingered Jack. For three years Joaquin Murieta, Three-Fingered Jack, Joaquin Valenzuela, Joaquin Carillo, Joaquin Claudio, Joaquin Ocomorenia, and Joaquin Botellier rampaged up and down

California, spreading terror everywhere.

No one knows how many Americans, killed in the night or along lonely daytime trails, fell victims of the bandits. Their teen-aged leader killed only for revenge. But Three-Fingered Jack, his principal lieutenant, was a cruel man who killed for the love of killing.

The bandits ravaged and plundered from Mount Shasta in the north to the Tehachapis in the south. But most of their attacks were in the Central California foothills from Marysville to Sonora. One incident reported in late 1851 is a good example of their work. Two men riding along the Feather River saw four Mexicans ahead, dragging an American who had been roped around the neck. Prudently minding their own business, the men hurried to find a sheriff. In the search that followed, six other murdered men were found near the same place on the trail. Each bore on his throat the burn marks of the lariat.

We don't know what happened to Rosita during the years of warfare. Some reports say she was killed; others say she dressed in men's clothing and traveled with her husband. Finally a panic-stricken citizenry called on Governor John Bigler to halt the slaughter.

In spring 1853 Bigler created a special company of California Rangers, headed by Harry Love, a former Texas Ranger and veteran of the war against Mexico. Love recruited the twenty best frontiersmen he could find. Good marksman of proven courage, they were all hard riders and as skilled at living in the open as the outlaws they pursued. The governor set a thousand dollar reward for Murieta and gave the rangers three months to bring him in, dead or alive.

On July 25 the rangers caught up with Murieta's band at Arroyo Cantina in the Kettleman Hills, near Coalinga. In a wild battle on horseback, the rangers killed four bandits, including Murieta and Three Fingered Jack. They cut off Murieta's head and Three Fingered Jack's deformed hand to prove their right to the reward. They brought their gruesome trophies, preserved in alcohol, to Stockton where they were put on public display before being moved to a museum in San Francisco.

Murieta's head was last seen rolling down an aisle after falling from its shelf in the 1906 earthquake.

Suggested reading: Walter Noble Burns, *The Robin Hood of El Dorado* (New York: Coward-McCann, 1932).

HANGING AN ANGEL

Paula Angel's outlaw career lasted only a few weeks, but it brought her a horrible death and her territory everlasting shame.

Nineteen-year-old Paula, the beauty of Las Vegas, New Mexico, came from a poor but proud old Spanish family of Conquistadors. She fell in love with Juan Miguel Martin, whose wealthy family wielded great power in Santa Fe.

In the early 1860s Las Vegas had the worst reputation in the southwest. Killers and robbers, run out of other states and territories, came there to hide from the law. Bawdy houses, gambling dens, and cantinas that never closed served the renegades of the frontier.

Soon after Martin conquered Paula, he tired of her and began spending long nights in cantinas where lovely señoritas, wearing little more than smiles, entertained young men on the prod for adventure.

One March evening in 1861 Martin and Paula had their first quarrel. She was appalled that he could be unfaithful when she had given him the most prized possession of all.

"Your fine words meant nothing," she said, tears streaming down her face. "You never intended that we should marry. You spend all your time on the *Sodomia La Calle de la Amargura* (street of suffering and bitterness)."

Martin pleaded with her for another chance. His torrent of endearments ended with a promise to see the priest and start publication of the wedding banns. Listening to her heart and not her head, Paula believed him, forgave him. Once again they parted as lovers.

Paula sang all the next morning as she went about her housework. Soon she would be *Señora* Martin, taking her place as mistress of a fine home in the respectable — although small — part of the town.

But when dusk fell and she had neither seen nor heard from her lover, she knew the ugly truth. Martin had made a fool of her again! He was shallow, unreliable, an animal among women! Paula wrapped her father's bowie knife in her shawl and took to the street.

She crouched in the shadows outside the *Cantina Gallinas*, one of Martin's hangouts. As she listened to the music and ribald laughter, tears worked their way down her ashen face. When a family friend came by, she asked him to tell Martin that she wanted to talk.

Martin swaggered out, half drunk. He scolded Paula for coming to that part of town.

"Let us speak the truth," Paula demanded. "Your promise of marriage was untrue, yes?" Her voice was hollow for she knew the answer.

"I'm not taking a peon's plaything like you into my family."

Paula stared speechless. He put his hands on her shoulders, leaned over and hissed, "You little fool."

Paula drew the knife swiftly. It slipped into him as easily as if his stomach were her mother's molded butter. Martin cried out and bent over in pain. The plunge into his back took more strength, but no more than cutting meat from a butchered animal. Paula stepped back, dazed, and men hurried to take the knife from her trembling hands.

Paula was held in solitary confinement to keep her away from the drunks and derelicts chained to the mud walls of the adobe jail. Three lawyers came from Santa Fe to prosecute her for murder. Paula's family hired Spruce Baird, fluent in two languages, to defend. Baird pleaded in Spanish and English that Paula was only defending her honor from a brute. But the jury said guilty.

Every morning Sheriff Antonio Herrera greeted her, "Paula I am going to hang you by the neck until you are dead, dead, dead." Then he would remind her of the number of days remaining until the execution date, April 26.

But the town didn't share the sheriff's contempt. When the hanging day came, most of its citizens, and even people from the Pecos River settlements, gathered at the large cottonwood tree on the Gallinas River. They saw the hangman's noose suspended from a limb, just over the wagon road. The sheriff drove up with Paula in his wagon. He adjusted the noose over her head. The watching crowd muttered. There would be no merciful, neck-breaking drop for Paula Angel. The sheriff would drive the wagon forward, and she would swing and strangle to death.

Paula stood silently as Herrera made final adjustments in the noose. She seemed weak, so he did not bind her arms. But when he drove the team forward he heard the crowd's hoarse gasp. He turned around to see the girl twisting, her small hands desperately clutching the rope above her head.

Herrera swore, jumped out of the wagon and ran back. He seized one of Paula's legs and yanked with his full weight, trying to break her grip on the rope. Paula kicked him with her other foot. Herrera's deputy grabbed the free foot and added his weight to the hanging girl. As Paula's hands started to slip and the noose tighten, an onlooker rushed forward, drew his knife and slashed the rope in two.

Paula fell to the ground, gasping for air. Bystanders told her to run, but she was too weak to stand. Herrera and the deputy lifted her into the wagon, tied the rope ends together, and readjusted the noose.

Two thousand people voiced their disapproval. "You have already hanged her once," someone shouted. "That satisfies the law."

"The court ordered her hanged until dead," Herrera shouted back. "Get out of the way."

Men rushed the wagon. They held the wheels and the check reins on the horses. Herrera frothed with rage.

"I have armed deputies among you," the sheriff yelled. "If you oppose due process of law, they will shoot."

Colonel J. D. Sena of the New Mexico Volunteers was present as a representative of the Martin family. They had demanded the death of Paula.

"A prominent young man has been murdered," Sena said. "The girl must die in expiation."

"She has been hanged once," an onlooker replied. "To hang her again is unjust and against the will of God."

"Let her go," chanted the crowd.

Herrera ordered his deputies to draw their guns. Colonel Sena was knocked from the wagon box and dragged into the crowd. One deputy held Paula up while another tied her hands behind her back and placed the noose around her neck. Other deputies smashed pistol barrels against hands holding wagon wheels. Bruised and bloody, the hands slowly let go.

The crowd turned its attention to Colonel Sena as his battered body absorbed kicks and stompings. Herrera took advantage of the distraction to seize his whip and bring it down on his team. The horses lunged forward.

Paula swung free a second time. Her limbs contracted, and horrible sounds came from her cloth-hooded head as she slowly and painfully strangled to death.

Paula Angel was the first woman legally hanged in New Mexico. She was also the last.

Suggested reading: Maurice Kildare, "The Hanging of Paula Angel" in *Real West* (V. 10, No. 55, Sept., 1967).

THE DIFFERENT ONE

Clay Allison was unique among western gunmen. People argued whether he was a villain or a gentleman, but all agreed that no other was like him. Liquor made the difference. Sober, he behaved himself. Women liked the tall, slender man, handsome as Apollo, with cold blue eyes under dark eyebrows. Strong drink changed him into a fearless fanatic who gloried in weird behavior.

The Jekyll-Hyde personality may have had biological causes which liquor aggravated. Allison's medical discharge from the Confederate Army referred to physical or emotional excitement which caused epileptic and maniacal problems. At war's end he moved to Texas and then on to New Mexico, where he ranched in Colfax County.

Most gunfighters had killed several men by the time they were out of their teens; Allison did not start until he was almost thirty.

One of his early killings showed the kind of bizarre conduct that made normal gunfighters hold him in superstitious dread. A rancher's wife had complained about her husband to Allison while Allison was in his cups. The husband had been arrested for murder, but no one was sure yet that anyone had been killed. Allison broke into the jail, dragged the woman's husband to a nearby tree, and hanged him. Then he cut off the victim's head, impaled it on a pole, and carried it twenty-nine miles to Cimarron, where he displayed his gruesome trophy in his favorite saloon.

Most gunfighters rode quickly out of town after they killed. Not Allison. Early in his career he killed five Black soldiers in a saloon. Then he paced the floor, hoping someone would come after him. No one did.

One of Allison's favorite amusements was to ride into a town, shooting out windows with a pistol in each hand. He varied the routine once in Canadian, Texas. He rode in almost naked, wearing only his hat and boots, his guns blazing.

Allison resembled other gunfighters in one respect; he was vengeful. Once he was beaten by three men and left for dead. He recovered and searched the West to track them down. Six months later he had killed them all.

Allison's sense of humor was grotesque. Once he trailed a herd of cattle to Cheyenne, Wyoming, arriving with a toothache. He went to one of the town's two dentists, but the man started drilling the wrong tooth. Allison jumped up

CLAY ALLISON

Western History Collections, University of Oklahoma Libraries

and ran to the other dentist to have the damage repaired and the correct tooth pulled. Then he returned to the first dentist, pinned him in his own chair, and extracted one of the dentist's teeth. He was working on a second extraction when the victim's screams brought help.

Allison's growing reputation as a gunfighter brought challenges from others. Chunk Colbert, who claimed seven victims at the time, wanted the prestige of making Allison the eighth. He invited his target to eat with him at the Red River Station in Colfax County. When the coffee was brought, Chunk reached for his cup with his left hand while he drew his pistol under the table with his right. Allison shoved the table into Chunk, forcing his shot to go wild. Allison fired as he fell over backward, hitting Chunk between the eyes.

Allison, with professional pride, often referred to himself as a shootist.

Allison's reputation for fearless, weird conduct led good gunmen to avoid him. Once he came to Dodge City, seeking a fight with Bat Masterson, one of the most skilled and efficient peace officers in the West. Bat was in town, but nobody could find him until after Allison left.

Another man faced Allison in a confrontation that was talked about far and wide, although neither man was killed. Mace Bowman and Allison got into a heated argument in a saloon. They laid their pistols side by side on the bar and backed off ten feet to see who could run and shoot the fastest. Allison won. Bowman, seeing he was coming in second, bared his chest in a heroic pose and said, "Shoot and be damned." Allison laid down his pistol, hugged Bowman, and set up another round of drinks.

In summer 1887, when Allison was in his late thirties, he had a dispute with a neighbor. They decided to jointly dig a deep grave and descend into it naked, each with a bowie knife. Whoever climbed out would have the tombstone engraved for the other. But this unusual encounter was one that Allison did not live long enough to complete.

Even in death, Allison was different. Most gunfighters were shot or hanged. On July 1, 1887, while he was hauling supplies to his ranch, drunk, Allison fell out of his wagon. A wheel ran over his neck, breaking it and killing him.

Suggested reading: George Hendricks, *The Bad Man of the West* (San Antonio: The Naylor Co., 1959).

JUST DISPENSATION

No one knows how many men Sam Brown killed in Texas before he moved to California. His California killings started in 1853 when he shot down a man in Mariposa. The next year he killed three more in Fiddletown, farther north. For that he served five years in San Quentin. Upon release he went to the Comstock country of Nevada.

Sam was big, dirty and quarrelsome. The expression about having a man for breakfast came from his boasting. He spent the 1859-60 winter in Genoa, at the foot of the Sierras, southwest of Carson City. Mark Twain, working on the *Territorial Enterprise* in nearby Virginia City, said the first twenty-six graves there contained murdered men, and Sam Brown was the worst desperado of them all.

Timid men ducked into stores or crossed the street when they saw the pathological killer approaching. When Sam entered a saloon, the saloon keeper dropped whatever he was doing — even if waiting on the richest man in camp — to see what Sam wanted. To challenge Sam was to court death.

Before 1859 was out, Sam picked on a drifter named Bill Bilboa in Carson City. He knocked the man down, beat him, and killed him with two pistol shots. Sam, seeing Bilboa in the street, had shouted for him to get out of the way, and didn't think Bilboa moved fast enough. Suddenly, Sam was acknowledged as the meanest man in the Comstock. He strutted around Carson City saloons, boasting of the men he had killed.

A short time later Sam was in a saloon when a drunk made a remark which offended him. He wound his muscular arm around the victim, holding him as easily as a cat holds a mouse. He drew his bowie knife and drove it twice into the quivering body, twisting it "Maltese fashion" into the vitals. Then he flung the bleeding body to the floor, laid down on a bench and calmly went to sleep as the blood poured from the dead man. Rumors spread that Sam had over a dozen notches in his pistol and about half that many in his knife.

The next summer Sam was working at a roadhouse when a man entered, saying he wanted something to eat. Sam pointed to a hanging strip of bacon. "Help yourself," he grunted.

"Could I borrow your knife to cut a slice?"

Sam pulled out his knife and then slid it back into his boot. "I've killed five men with that knife," he said, smiling strangely. "Don't know as I want to lend it out to cut bacon." The man left quickly and quietly, deciding to eat elsewhere.

Like the lion which singles out the weakest for its kill, Sam was careful to select his victims where there would be no reprisals. But Sam met two determined foes in his short lifetime. He backed down from the first, and tried unsuccessfully to hide from the second.

The first determined man was William C. Stewart, a six feet, two, 200-pound man with piercing blue eyes and ambition to match his courage and strength. On his own at fourteen, Stewart had dropped out of Yale to head west in the gold rush. He had been a district attorney and the state Attorney General in California before moving to the Comstock. Nevadans would later send him to the United States Senate.

Bill Stewart had been asked to arbitrate a mining dispute. He held the hearing in a small room behind a bar, where several witnesses were waiting to testify. When Sam swaggered in, saying "swear me," Bill drew two loaded derringers, pointed them at Sam's chest and told his assistant to swear the witness. Sam testified quickly, politely, and was glad to return to the bar, unhurt.

When the hearing ended and Stewart walked out to the bar, Sam was still there.

"Damn you," Sam said to Stewart, "I like your kind. Have a drink." During their discussion, Sam said he needed a fighting lawyer to represent him in some litigation in the Aurora mining camp.

"I believe you and me, working together, can get some justice down there," Sam said.

Stewart agreed, naming his retainer. Sam said he'd have it in a day or two. He left with Alexander Henderson to ride somewhere for supper.

"It's my thirtieth birthday," Sam told his companion. "I need me a man for supper."

After stopping at two road houses where everyone seemed well-armed and prepared, Sam decided to ride to Van Sickle's. That's when he met the second determined man.

Henry Van Sickle was a Dutchman from New Jersey. He had been an Indian fighter, a bullwhacker during the California gold rush, and had been in Genoa for nine years. By training, he was a blacksmith. He had patiently built up his station, consisting of five barns, a dance hall, bar, several sleeping rooms, kitchen, dining room, and smithy. He mined

16

his own rock to build the station. It was celebrated on the emigrant trail for its hospitality and for the stability and honesty of its owner. Van Sickle had served as justice of the peace, and would later be a county commissioner and county treasurer.

"I've come to kill you, you sonofabitch," Sam told Van Sickle when the Dutchman came out to stable Sam's horse.

Van Sickle, knowing Brown's reputation, turned and ran. He fled through his dining room, where twenty men were eating supper.

"Where'd the sonofabitch go?" shouted Brown when he reached the dining room. But then he shrugged, holstered his gun, and returned to his horse to ride away.

Van Sickle got his double barreled shotgun, mounted a fast horse, and chased after Brown. He caught up in about a mile. He shouted to Brown's riding companion to get out of the way, and fired two shots. Both missed. Van Sickle reloaded, fired both barrels again, this time knocking off Sam's hat. By now the Dutchman was out of ammunition, although Sam didn't know that.

Sam, who had no stomach for that kind of fighting, took cover in Bill Cosser's house. Van Sickle's friends caught up with him, bringing more ammunition. Sam galloped on up the road, Van Sickle still in pursuit. Near Mrs. Mott's house, another exchange of shots had no effect. Sam took cover in the house.

It was getting dark, and Van Sickle feared that Sam would get away. Learning that Sam had slipped out of the Mott house, Van Sickle rode on ahead and reached Luther Old's station just ahead of Sam. He heard Sam's spurs jingle in the darkness as he dismounted.

"Now I kills you," the Dutchman shouted, running out to the road to meet Sam. His two shotgun slugs in the chest were his birthday present to the most savage killer ever to terrorize the Comstock.

At the inquest the next day, the coroner's jury said Sam Brown had come to his death from a just dispensation of an all-wise Providence.

Henry Van Sickle, the man who had hunted down his prey to kill him, was freed from custody.

Suggested reading: Daniel L. Reardon, "The Despicable Sam Brown," in *Frontier Times, v. 39, no. 6,* (Oct.- Nov., 1965).

WARM, INSIDE WORK

We only know the name of the wizened little Chinese man as Yu. He was seen near the store in Pioneer, Montana Territory, that winter night in 1872-73 when the store was broken into. The safe was broken open and a good supply of money stolen. Yu didn't do it, but he had no alibi, and he knew who did. The culprit was a Chinese friend with a large family to support.

The jury pronounced Yu guilty. That night he had a long visit from another Chinese, during which an official-looking document in Chinese writing was executed. The jailer was puzzled at the goings-on, and even more puzzled at Yu's calm manner the next day when they took him to the state penitentiary to begin his sentence.

Yu was assigned to the kitchen, and he became a model prisoner. A Deer Lodge newspaper said he "reveled in dishwater like a maid among the coral groves."

Yu never complained. He seemed to appreciate having a warm room and a dry roof over his head with an easy task to perform. He also appreciated knowing that three dollars a day was being paid to the person he had designated according to the terms of the contract executed that night in the jail.

The truth came out at the end of his three-year sentence. Nowhere else could a Chinese man make twenty-one dollars a week in a job that steady and easy with no temptation to spend his money on rotgut whiskey.

The newspaper said the humiliation of penitentiary service rested easily on Yu's conscience whenever he remembered that he would have enough money saved to return to China when his term ended.

"After all," said the newspaper — following the thinking of the times — "One Chinee would do as good as another."

Suggested reading: Fred Harrison, *Hell Holes and Hangings* (Clarendon, Texas: Clarendon Press, 1968).

THE ORIGINAL BILLY THE KID

Billy the Kid wasn't the Robin Hood of the West, and he didn't kill twenty-one men — not including Indians — by the time he, himself, was killed at twenty-one. A juvenile thief, he became a juvenile murderer. He assumed the name William H. Bonney. The first name came from his stepfather; no one knows where the surname came from. People called him Billy the Kid, but he was not the first to use that name.

William H. Bonney did kill about a half dozen men. Most were unarmed and shot from ambush. He didn't die with his boots on when his former friend and outlaw partner, Sheriff Pat Garrett, shot him down on July 14, 1881. Garrett gave Billy the same chance Billy had given his victims. He shot the Kid without warning in a bedroom in Pete Maxwell's place at Fort Summer. Billy was in his stocking feet.

The transformation of a two bit outlaw into a cult hero shows the power of some writers' imaginations and the gullibility of their readers. But part of the reason for the folklore that Billy the Kid was really a misunderstood juvenile came from the honest mistake of a Catholic nun, Sister Blandina Segale, one of the finest women in the American Southwest.

You see, the Billy the Kid that Sister Blandina knew was really Billy LeRoy, the first of a long line of hoodlums to use the name, Billy the Kid. After seeing Billy the Kid (LeRoy) several times, Sister Blandina heard that Billy the Kid (Bonney) had been killed. She mistakenly wrote that Bonney was the man she knew.

In 1876 Sister Blandina nursed a wounded member of Billy LeRoy's gang for four months, restoring him to health. He wondered if God would forgive him for his life of crime. She reminded him of the thief, crucified with Christ, who heard the words, "This day thou shalt be with me in paradise." Billy's partner wasn't so sure. During one of the visits to the wounded man, she met Billy LeRoy. She described LeRoy as young, about seventeen, innocent-looking, with a peach complexion and steel-blue eyes.

A grateful LeRoy told Sister, "Anytime my pals and I can serve you, you will find us ready."

The LeRoy gang had threatened to scalp all four of the physicians in Trinidad, Colorado. One of them, Dr. Michael Beshoar, served the Sister's convent. She asked the gang to leave the doctors alone. They agreed.

Two years later, after Sister had been transferred to Santa Fe, LeRoy and his gang were terrorizing the Santa Fe Trail. Sister Blandina was a passenger in a stage which LeRoy stopped with drawn pistol. When he recognized Sister he raised his hat, bowed, and rode away, stopping long enough to entertain the passengers with fancy maneuvers on his broncho.

Three years after that Sister Blandina visited LeRoy and one of his men in the Santa Fe jail. LeRoy, chained hand and foot and fastened to the floor, said gallantly, "I wish I could offer you a chair, Sister."

When she learned that Billy the Kid had been shot by Pat Garrett, Sister Blandina wrote, "Only now have I learned Billy the Kid's proper name, William H. Bonney."

She was wrong. The Billy she knew was Billy LeRoy, a Colorado outlaw who had worked for a time as a female impersonator in Leadville. He was a year older than Bonney but looked very young. He was blue-eyed and slim, with an innocent, boyish face.

Sister wrote about knowing Billy the Kid in letters to Sister Justina Segale, who was also a Sister of Charity as well as Sister Blandina's blood sister back in Ohio. The letters have been published in Sister Blandina's book, *At The End of the Santa Fe Trail* (Columbus: The Columbian Press, 1932.)

Beside the similarities in the appearances of the two men, another circumstance helped keep the true facts concealed for about fifty years. Pat Garrett shot Bonney on July 14, 1881. LeRoy had been killed on May 24 the same year.

LeRoy teamed up with his brother Sam and another bandit to hold up the Del Norte-Lake City stage in a lonesome canyon of the Rio Grande in Colorado. The other robber was Bill Miner, one of the most famous robbers in history. Miner escaped; the LeRoy brothers were captured.

The brothers were convicted and each sentenced to ten years of hard labor. They never served their sentences. A lynch mob overpowered the jailers and hung both Billy LeRoy, the original Billy the Kid, and his brother, Sam.

So the mistake of a Catholic nun contributed to the folklore that one of the West's worst hoodlums was really an nice young man, caught up in a bitter feud as he fought to help his friends.

Suggested reading: Don Cline, "Billy LeRoy: The Original Billy the Kid in *Frontier Times, v. 56, no. 3* (Feb., 1985).

PERILS WHEN MOUNTED

Dick Fellows came from a distinguished Kentucky family, proud of its horsemanship skill. But Dick, California's most unsuccessful robber, should have waited for the automobile before taking up crime.

Dick, who used his true name, George Lytle, only when posing as a professor of languages, was a short, muscular man with a glib tongue and a rare sense of humor. Wells Fargo's chief detective considered him as daring a man as he had ever chased.

Dick began his career at age twenty-three in 1869 when he robbed a lone horseman near Los Angeles. Then he robbed a stagecoach near Santa Barbara, escaping with considerable plunder. He was on foot for the two holdups.

Captured shortly after the stage holdup, Dick was sentenced to San Quentin. He persuaded the prison officials that he was an experienced academic, and he got a cushy job in the prison library. He was soon lecturing his fellow felons on world history and literature. He organized a bible class, convinced California Governor Newton Booth that he was a born-again Christian, and won a pardon.

"I'm through with crime forever," Dick vowed as reporters interviewed him, walking out the gate.

His resolve ended a year later as he stood in Caliente, the end of the rail line running south from San Francisco toward Los Angeles. Goods had to be transferred at that point from trains to complete their journey by stagecoach. Dick watched as a quarter of a million dollars in gold coin was being moved from car to coach. He decided to gallop ahead and intercept the stage on a quiet roadway. All he needed was a horse.

He had no trouble renting the animal; the trouble was staying in the saddle. He rode happily out of Caliente, remembering that his Kentucky relatives were superb horsemen. But two miles down the road, the horse reared, got rid of Dick, and returned to town.

Dick picked himself up, shook off the dust, walked back to Caliente, and changed his plans. Now he would rob the incoming stage from Los Angeles, due that evening. Dick, as stubborn as he was brave, decided to use a different horse this time. The first one was back in the livery barn, but he saw another, tied in front of a store, and he took it without asking.

Dick rode out, met the stage, drew his gun, and ordered the driver to throw down the treasure box. Then he realized that he had nothing which he could use to open the locked box. He had to get the heavy box out of the roadway, so he tried to lift it up to the saddle and balance it there while he got aboard. It didn't work. The horse reared and ran away.

By then it was dark and Dick had no time to ponder why two horses had abandoned him in the same day. He knew he must move fast. He had seen railroad construction along the roadway, and he thought the high piles of rock and dirt, where a tunnel was being drilled, would provide cover. He hoisted the box to his shoulder and started over a dark, unfamiliar path.

He plunged over a precipice, landing in an excavation eighteen feet below. When he came to, he found his left ankle broken and the foot crushed. He worked painfully most of the night to hide the treasure box. Then he crawled to a tent containing Chinese railroad workers. He stole an axe and used it to open the box. Now he had $1800 in gold coin!

Dick cut crutches from forked willows and walked to another part of the camp, where he bought food with some of his stolen money. He hid out until the next evening, and then headed for a distant farmhouse. He stole a horse from a field and was on his way, a mounted man again!

Unknown to Dick, his mount had recently lost a shoe. It had been replaced with a mule shoe. Between the farmer's son tracking down the horse, and Wells Fargo's detective working at the scene of the holdup, Dick was soon captured. He persuaded the Bakersfield judge to give him just eight years in San Quentin this time.

But when the astonished jailer opened the cell to transfer Dick to prison, he saw a large hole in the wall and no Dick.

Dick's freedom didn't last long. He hobbled to a barn on his crutches and hid. When hunger drove him to desperate measures, he stole another horse and tried to ride away. He was quickly thrown and quickly recaptured.

Back in San Quentin, Dick taught ethics and morals to fellow convicts. Good conduct shortened his sentence to five years. Upon release he went to Santa Cruz and advertised in the newspaper that Professor George Lytle was again accepting students in his Spanish classes.

The ads soon stopped, and Dick returned to his first love, making roadside withdrawals from Wells Fargo accounts.

Bad luck continued to plague him. His holdup of a stage near Santa Cruz netted an almost empty express box. It contained only a single letter, and that was written in Chinese. The newspapers began carrying reports of a daring lone stagecoach bandit working in the area.

After months of robberies, Dick was captured again. He was tried in Santa Barbara County and got life, this time in Folsom Prison.

But the day before Dick was to be transferred from the jail to Folsom, he escaped for his last time. He knocked the turnkey to the floor and fled with the officer's gun.

Dick saw a horse grazing next to the jail. Without time to ponder his life experiences with horses, Dick leaped aboard the unsaddled horse and hung on for dear life. They had gone only a short distance when the horse collapsed and rolled over on the ground in a fit. Dick learned, on his way back to Folsom, that the animal had been eating loco weed and had been staked out on grass to recover.

Thirty-three years later — it was 1915, the year of the Panama-Pacific Exposition in San Francisco — a stooped, gray-haired man walked into the sheriff's office in Santa Barbara.

"Is Judge Smith still alive?" he asked. "I was once a friend of his."

"What's your name?"

"I was once known as Dick Fellows."

The sheriff remembered him and shook hands warmly. "Do you have a job?" he asked.

"I'm in charge of the Kentucky state exhibit at the exposition in San Francisco," Dick said proudly.

"I suppose you'll have something in your exhibit about those great Kentucky thoroughbreds," the sheriff said. "Fine horsemen, those Kentuckians."

"Might do it," Dick grinned ruefully.

Suggested reading: Eugene B. Block, *Great Stagecoach Robbers of the West* (Garden City: Doubleday & Company, 1962).

THE LAST ESCAPE

The Pinkerton Detective Agency called Bill Miner the master criminal of the American West. He robbed his first California stage at age sixteen. Three years later, he got the first of his four sentences to San Quentin. He assured his place in history at age fifty-seven with the first train robbery in Canada. At age sixty-four, he robbed a train in Georgia.

A slender man, about five feet nine and 130 pounds, Miner was good looking and intelligent. He was known for the steely look in his cold, blue eyes. Born in Kentucky and fairly well educated, Miner had a southern hospitality and charm. He usually apologized in a soft drawl to the passengers of the stages he robbed, "Sorry for the inconvenience, folks." When he finished robbing a train, he often admonished the engineer to drive carefully to the nearest station.

Miner became as well known for his escapes as for the polite way he relieved stages and trains of their money and their passengers of their valuables. None of his escapes lasted long. He was usually back in custody in a day or two. But the number of escapes and the imagination displayed were memorable.

Nothing unusual marked Miner's first escape. Within hours he was caught, beaten, and thrown into the prison dungeon. He had been in San Quentin's infamous dungeon before. The tiny cells, dug out of solid rock, had no beds, no lights, no sunshine, no ventilation. Three to four men shared each cell. A wooden bucket toilet and a concrete block chair were the only facilities. The prisoners got bread and water at the whim of the guards. If they made too much noise, the guards spread lime on the damp floor, wet it down, and let acrid, suffocating fumes subdue their unruly charges.

Miner's first legal release was in 1880, after he had served thirteen years. Surprisingly, his brutal treatment had not embittered him. He cowboyed through New Mexico to Denver, where he assumed a new name, posing as a distinguished southern gentleman. His courtly manner charmed the ladies. A free spender in the saloons, he probably mixed some stage robbing into his cowboying.

Before the year was out, Miner and two confederates held up a stage in southwestern Colorado. They got $3600 in gold dust and coin. After apologizing to the passengers for the ten-minute delay and cautioning the driver to go carefully on the treacherous road, the robbers split up.

The confederates, Billy and Sam Leroy, were caught and hanged. By Christmas Miner had turned up in Michigan.

He charmed the ladies for a few months, even becoming engaged to one. But his money ran out, and he returned to Colorado to rob another stage. Soon captured, Miner escaped from the sheriff and two deputies who held him. His four shots in the blazing getaway struck an officer each time.

He reached Arizona on stolen horses. Soon, Arizona stage drivers began hearing the soft-spoken command, "Hands Up," by then Miner's trademark.

By fall, Miner was back in California. In early November he held up the Sonora-Milton stage. In December he got twenty-five years in San Quentin.

Four years later, Miner escaped. Captured in a few hours, he was thrown into the dungeon. He stayed so long this time, the guards considered him a fixture.

In 1901, after serving 19 years of his sentence, Miner was paroled at age 54. The solitary confinement, the beatings, the lung-eating gases from wet lime had not broken him. His soft voice and polite smile concealed a determination to continue his life of crime. He went northwest with a new name.

Few stages still ran. Trains now carried the gold. Old Bill Miner took in a 19-year-old partner and started a second career of robbing trains. In fall 1903 Miner and his small gang robbed a train near Portland. Most of the gang was captured, but not Miner. He crossed into Canada, where his charm and education led him into the social life of a small community.

A year later, near Vancouver, a soft-spoken, "Hands Up," started Canada's first train robbery. No one suspected the charming "George Edwards," but the Pinkerton Agency added more information to its file on the master criminal in the American West.

George Edwards continued to impress people as a southern gentleman of leisure, with now even more money.

Two years later, three masked men, one of them soft-spoken, held up a train in Washington. Edwards continued charming British Columbia citizens. His money bought candy for the children and other gifts for the adults.

The following spring, Miner and two confederates robbed a British Columbia train. After a short flight, they were captured, convicted, and Miner got life in prison. As the constable led him away, the 59-year-old spoke softly to one of the Crown's witnesses:

"If I'm ever in the area again, I'll look you up."

Age seemed to have caught up with Miner. The warden's

daughter brought him religious books, and the prison, satisfied that the lame old man no longer planned escape, assigned him to the brickyard. No one thought it unusual when the old man always stopped at the same place along the wall as he pushed his wheel barrow back for a fresh load. The guards thought he was tired and needed a rest. Other inmates soon realized that the old man was slowly digging a tunnel under the wall, spreading the dirt around so it would not be noticed. Eventually three other inmates were resting with their wheel barrows at the same place. The tunnel was soon completed.

After the four men had crawled through the tunnel, they climbed over the outer wall, using a ladder found by Miner. Back in Seattle, the Pinkertons wearily re-opened their Miner file and sent descriptions throughout the United States. The three confederates were soon captured, but Miner stayed hidden for three years.

Then, in 1910, Miner and two young confederates held up the first train in Georgia. The two younger men, soon captured, confessed and got fifteen years each. Miner was also arrested, but the local police did not think the tired, lame old man could be a train robber. A Pinkerton man noticed Miner in his cell and soon identified him from his tattoos. Miner was sentenced to 20 years.

Seven months later, taking a young confederate with him, Miner escaped again. They eluded bloodhounds for seventeen days. Then, in a shootout with police, the confederate was killed and Miner gave up.

The guards took no chances with the old man this time. He was sick and weak, but they put a ball and chain on him anyway. In 1912 Miner sawed through his shackles, cut the bars from his cell and escaped into a swamp. He was nearly out of his head when he staggered from the swamp into the arms of the posse. Poisonous snakes and the lack of any houses to rob for food were too much for him.

On September 2, 1913, Bill Miner died. The newspapers said it was his third escape from a Georgia prison, this time accompanied by the angel of death. No relatives could be found. The townspeople put up the money for the funeral, and hundreds filed past the casket. Even in death, Bill Miner attracted friends.

Suggested reading: Frank W. Anderson, *Bill Miner, Train Robber* (Calgary: Frontier Publishing, 1968).

THE BENDER MYSTERY

Kate Bender, her sixty-year-old parents, and her half-witted brother, John, showed up in southeastern Kansas in 1871. They built a small cabin and a sod barn near the Osage Mission Trail.

Old man Bender hung a crudely-lettered sign, "Groceries," over the front door. Not many people stopped at the rustic inn. Some who did were never seen again.

Kate claimed mystic powers.

"I kin see spirits and hear voices other people caint," she advertised. "My guide is an old Indian chief. He and me kin cure all kinds of diseases in our see-ances. Blindness, fits, deafness and all sech. Also deaf and dumbness."

In spring 1872 Kate got part-time work as a waitress in a small hotel in Cherryvale. She gave lectures on spiritualism in her off hours.

One day a neighborhood farmer stopped at the Bender store. "They didn't seem to know who I was at first," the farmer told his friends. "I walked inside and the girl there had a surprised look on her face when she recognized me. Jist then the old man stepped out from behind the door. Had a sledgehammer in his hand, he did. Seemed odd to me. I sure didn't hear any pounding as I was walking up. They's something powerful strange about that place."

Father Paul Ponziglione, stationed at the mission, stopped at Bender's one night during a thunderstorm.

"I had this terrible nervous feeling," Father Paul reported. "It didn't just seem right there, somehow. I couldn't get to sleep. Then this big bolt of lightning struck, and thunder shook the house something fierce. I was out of that bed, got my clothes on, and was out the door and on my horse, galloping away, before you could say Hail Mary!"

Father Paul's experience fanned growing rumors that the Bender store was a weird place.

Crazy old Julie Hesler, who always carried a shotgun, helped the rumors along. Fascinated by spiritualism, she called on Kate one night.

"They had pichers of men all over the walls," she said. "They was sticking knives right into them. Kate told me that sometimes the spirits told her to kill. Then her nose sorta twitched like a cat pouncing on a mouse and her lips was drawed back tight and she whispered that they was telling her to kill me right then. I jumped up, grabbed old Betsey here and got outa there quickern scat!" She cackled and patted her shotgun. "I didn't stop till I was to home and had my doors locked. I tell you, it give me the cold shivers right up my backbone."

Doctor William York, a prominent politician and member of the Kansas legislature, disappeared in March, 1873. He had been visiting his brother, a colonel at Fort Scott, and was following the mission trail to his home in Independence. When the doctor vanished, his brother traced him to the Bender store.

"Shore he stopped here," Kate said, smiling mysteriously. "I remember him. He made a small purchase — I don't rightly remember jist what — and then he rode on."

The colonel's visit may have frightened the Benders, for they, too, vanished. The neighbors who came to investigate found Doctor York's body in a shallow grave in the Bender fruit orchard. His throat had been cut and his skull crushed. Eleven more graves were soon found.

The Bender team, wagon, and dog were found at Thayer, fifteen miles north. The Thayer railroad agent remembered selling tickets to two men and two women for transportation to Humboldt, twenty-five miles further north. The trail ended there. No one knows where the Benders came from to Kansas; no one knows where they went.

Many persons seeking reflected limelight from the mystery claimed knowledge of the Benders afterward. One story appeared in a Topeka newspaper in August, 1877. It said that a Captain Don Pieppo was sailing a small vessel from Mexico to Galveston in April, 1873. As his ship was being battered by a strong northwest wind, he heard voices from the Heavens. He looked up to see something entangled on his mast. It was a gondola, containing two men and two women.

The women and the older man were killed in the crash, but the younger man was still alive. The young man gave the name John Bender. He said the four of them had escaped from Kansas in a balloon filled with natural gas from a boiling spring. They had floated across Indian Territory and Texas, but lost control of the balloon during the storm.

Captain Pieppo said John Bender died a few hours after the crash. Then the captain's ship sunk, carrying with it the four heavenly visitors.

Suggested reading: David Dary, *True Tales of the Old-Time Plains* (New York: Crown Publishers, 1979).

MAIL ORDER BRIDE

Two daily stages connected Colfax, California, on the Central Pacific Railroad, with the mining towns of Grass Valley and Nevada City. Only one stage ran on Sunday. On Sunday, July 23, 1873, eleven men and one woman boarded the stage at Colfax. The woman, Eleanor Webber, was coming west to marry a man she had never seen; they had met by correspondence. The Wells Fargo agent put almost eight thousand dollars in coin in the strong box, built into the back of the stage and cushioned for a seat. Driver Bob Scott shook his team into a trot as they headed down the curving road toward Bear River. Five miles short of Grass Valley, as the stage moved along at a walk, four masked men with double-barreled shotguns stepped out.

"What do you want?" asked Scott.

"Just the treasure box."

"It's coming on the other stage."

"Well, we'll keep you here until the other stage comes." The robber laughed. "Come on, we know it's Sunday. You and your passengers get on out. You unhitch your team."

The robbers herded the passengers down the road and ordered them to sit, cross-legged, in a row. They attacked the double-locked box with a pick, breaking the first lock. As they brought up a canister of powder and a fuse for the second lock, Eleanor Webber spoke up.

"Gentlemen, my trunk sitting by that seat contains everything I own in the world. It'll do you no good, but 'twill be an irreparable loss to me. I beg you to take it out before you blow the safe open."

The outlaw leader gallantly reassured Eleanor. He put his powder can down, lifted the trunk out, and handed it to a confederate, who carried it to safety. As the leader lifted the trunk, a gust of wind moved his mask, and the girl had a brief look at his face.

After the blast, the robbers gathered up the coins, and the leader put the trunk back into the shattered coach. "You can hitch up and go on," he said to the driver.

The running gear was undamaged, so Scott drove the battered stage and its passengers into Grass Valley. He made a special stop at the address given him by Eleanor. A woman came out of the house and told the girl that her fiance, a man named Louis Dreibelbis, had been called away on an emergency and could not be there to meet her. The other passengers noted that the girl seemed even more distraught than she had during the holdup.

Eleanor Webber's hostess assured the girl that Louis was expected momentarily.

"We've got the parlor all fixed up for the wedding," she said. "The preacher will come soon's I call. You just freshen yourself up and I'll get you something to eat and you'll feel better. We've been having so many stage robberies lately!"

After Eleanor had bathed, changed into fresh clothes, and had supper, her hostess announced that her betrothed had arrived, and the preacher was there, too. She led the expectant girl into the dimly lit parlor, where the clergyman and a witness were sitting with Eleanor's future husband.

The men rose as Eleanor and her hostess entered. Before the girl had a good look at her husband-to-be, the preacher started moving the bride, the groom, and the witnesses into their proper positions for the ceremony. Louis' voice seemed strangely familiar to Eleanor, but she was unable to place where she had heard it. For some reason — probably shyness, Eleanor thought — Louis did not embrace her and seemed to turn his face away.

The bride bowed her head demurely during the ceremony, making the correct responses. When the preacher was through, the couple drew together for the traditional kiss. Eleanor looked up at her new husband, and the light from the kerosene lamp fell full on his face. Her cry of outrage astonished the others in the room. She tore herself from Louis' arms and ran, sobbing convulsively, to her room. Panic-stricken, Louis Dreibelbis rushed out of the house.

Eleanor refused to come out of the room until her hostess had booked her passage on the next out-bound stage. Humiliated and embarrassed, she left Grass Valley forever.

About two weeks later James B. Hume, Wells Fargo detective, arrested Dreibelbis, tying him to the Grass Valley stage holdup as well as others. Dreibelbis, who also used the name, Robert Walker, was a well-educated man from Galena, Illinois. He came west to prospect and turned to crime when mining did not pay. He claimed that he had been a county sheriff in Illinois before he came to California.

Dreibelbis confessed and testified for the state in several trials that cleared up stage robberies. Hume provided him transportation back to his Illinois home. With that, history closed the curtain on Eleanor Webber and Louis Dreibelbis. Perhaps Louis tried again to write. Perhaps Eleanor got a divorce or annulment. Who knows?

Suggested reading: Richard Dillon, *Wells, Fargo Detective* (Reno: University of Nevada Press, 1986).

THOSE WHO LIVE BY THE SWORD

Sostenes l'Archevêque's grandfather Jean left France at twelve with the exploring expedition of Robert de La Salle. After the expedition had traveled down the Mississippi to its mouth, Jean l'Archevêque, by then sixteen, diverted La Salle's attention while another member of the crew murdered their leader.

Later Jean surrendered to the Spanish and then dropped out of sight for some years. By 1696 he had reached New Mexico, where he served in the army at the Presidio in Santa Fe. He was a member of the ill-fated Pedro de Villasur expedition of 1720, which reached further into the interior than any other Spanish expedition. Pawnees killed most of the explorers, including Jean, when they reached the Platte River.

Sostenes inherited his grandfather's love of violence and met an even more violent death. The grandson, a six-foot, four-inch, blue-eyed blonde, was called handsome by the señoritas. His mother was Mexican-Indian. He had seen his father killed by an American, and his hatred for gringos knew no bounds.

"When I grow up," he vowed, "I will kill every white man I meet."

By the mid 1870s the Canadian River Valley in the Texas Panhandle was the domain of Sostenes and Mexican sheepherders. But in 1876 two Casner brothers and a Navajo Indian boy trailed a large flock of sheep into the valley, looking for open range. The brothers had struck it rich with a California gold mine. They had invested some of their fortune in sheep, and, according to legend, carried the rest in bags filled with twenty-dollar gold pieces.

Sostenes decided to repel the invaders and rob them at the same time. Saying he was just going on a hunting trip, he persuaded Ysabel Gurules, a young Mexican boy, to go with him.

When they reached the sheep camp, only one brother was there. Sostenes talked with him long enough to learn that the other two were with the sheep. Then he shot the brother down in cold blood. A shocked Ysabel cried and pleaded with the assassin, but Sostenes slapped him and told him to hide, while he waited for the others.

As the second brother rode up, Sostenes shot him down without warning.

"Now you ride out and shoot the Indian kid, you little cry baby," Sostenes ordered Ysabel.

A trembling Ysabel jumped on a horse and escaped back to town. Sostenes met the Indian as he moved the flock in. He shoved his gun unto the boy's stomach. One of the sheep dogs leaped at the intruder, only to be shot in the head. Sostenes spun back to the Navajo boy with a final demand for the gold. The boy, paralyzed with fear, told where one bag was, saying he did not know about the rest. Sostenes beat him to death with his pistol. When a second dog attacked, he shot and killed it.

He left the gory scene and found a heavy leather bag filled with coins. Then he roped one of the dead brothers, dragged him to the edge of a cliff with his horse, and kicked the body into a canyon.

With the pistol of one of the brothers in his belt and his pockets filled with coins, he rode away. After hiding out a while, Sostenes rode into town. News of the first merciless killing had caused the citizens, including friends and relatives of the killer, to decide that he should be killed.

As Sostenes entered the house of Felix Gurules, Felix and another stabbed him in the back with a long knife. Then Colás Martínez, Sostenes' brother-in-law, stepped through a door and fired twice point-blank into the killer's body. It still took all three men to wrestle him to the floor. As Sostenes lay there, two men holding his hands and the other with a knee in his stomach, he screamed his defiance: "Pull that knife out of my back and I'll kill every one of you!"

A pistol blow to the head knocked him out temporarily. Then he kicked and screamed, calling down evil spirits on his attackers. One of the men choked him and the others continued to pistol-whip him. Not until one of them ripped the cross from Sostenes' neck did he pass out. He died the next morning.

A contemporary of Billy the Kid, Sostenes had killed even more men. But unlike the Kid, he had no friends and no principles to avenge. The most hated man in New Mexico and West Texas was killed by his own people. They buried him on the crest of a hill, near the Canadian River. The cross they put up has long since rotted away, but the place is still called *Sierrita de la Cruz* — Little Mountain of the Cross.

Suggested reading: John L. McCarty, *Maverick Town, the story of Old Tascosa* (Norman: U. of Okla. Press, 1968).

HELL IS IN SESSION IN CALDWELL

When James D. Sherman of DeKalb County, Missouri, asked for work at the Millett Brothers Ranch in the Texas Panhandle, he said his name was Jim Daniels. The Millett hands were notorious for gunfighting; Daniels looked the part and was hired.

He fit right in. When the sheriff and three deputies rode up in February, 1881, to arrest Daniels and three other hands for horse stealing, a gun battle followed. All four outlaws escaped, although Daniels was hit by shotgun fire. All four officers were wounded, but they survived.

Daniels followed a cattle herd up the Chisholm Trail to Caldwell, Kansas, a brawling trail town. With two warrants out for him in Texas, he decided to stay. His wife and two small children joined him from Texas. Now he said his name was Jim Talbot.

Some of Talbot's trail partners from the Millett Brothers Ranch also settled in Caldwell. They included Tom Love, Dick Eddleman, Bob Bigtree, Bob Munson, Doug Hill, and Jim Martin. Their troubles with the law in Caldwell began immediately and came to a head on December 17, 1881. On that day, a Wichita newspaper wrote, "As we go to press, Hell is in session in Caldwell."

The night before, Talbot and his friends, accompanied by what the local newspaper called "their prostitutes," went to a performance of Uncle Tom's Cabin. Their shouting and shooting disturbed the whole theater. The next morning they resumed their gunplay, accompanied by two local sports, George Speer and Comanche Bill Mankin. The city marshal enlisted help from local citizens, including former mayor, Mike Meagher.

Caldwell rumbled like a volcano that day. Skirmishes broke out here and there, finally erupting into a general gun battle which left Meagher and Speer dead in the streets. Another gun battle followed as the outlaws tried to reach their horses and get out of town.

Love and Eddleman were captured. The other five galloped out, hoping to reach Indian Territory. One of them has his horse killed under him. He jumped up behind one of his comrades, and they rode on, stopping long enough to steal a replacement horse from a man hauling hay into Caldwell.

By this time, dozens of irate citizens had joined the

chase after the outlaws. The fugitives stopped at a ranch south of town, hoping to replace their tired horses. But the posse rode too close behind them. With no time to move the saddles to fresh mounts, Talbot led the men to a stone dugout in the brush.

Three of the outlaws got into the dugout and quickly piled up more rocks into a breastworks. The other two took up concealed positions where they could ward off an attack on the dugout, and, at the same time, the men in the dugout could protect them.

Gunfire continued until dark. Several in the posse had been wounded. They posted guards around the dugout to keep up an all-night watch. When they moved in by morning light, they discovered that all five outlaws had slipped away. The posse could not even see signs that any of the men had been wounded.

In a remarkable aftermath to the session of Hell in Caldwell, the *Kansas City Times* published a letter signed by the five outlaws, writing from "in camp." They replied indignantly to news accounts setting out the citizens' side of the controversy. They insisted that they did not ride into town for the fight — they had already arrived; they were not mounted when they shot Meagher; Meagher was shooting with borrowed pistols; and the marshal was drunk.

Love was acquitted after a preliminary hearing in court. Eddleman, who had been captured with him, escaped.

Hill pleaded guilty to manslaughter and was sentenced to six months in jail. Nothing more was ever heard of Bigtree, Martin, or Munson. Talbot went on trial in 1895; the jury deadlocked.

In Talbot's second trial he was acquitted and he returned to his home, then in Ukiah, California. The next year he was killed by an unknown assassin, rumored to be his wife's lover.

Suggested reading: Nyle Miller & Joseph Snell, *Great Gunfighters of the Kansas Cowtowns, 1867-1886* (Lincoln: University of Nebraska Press, 1967).

LAME JOHNNY

When Cornelius Donahue graduated from Girard College in Philadelphia, he went west. Changing his name to John Hurley to shield his family from embarrassment, he struck out for Texas. An injury on a horse whem he was a boy left him with a lifelong limp and the name he was known by, Lame Johnny.

After cowboying in Texas he joined the 1876 rush to the Black Hills to try prospecting. He also served briefly, but well, as a deputy sheriff of Custer County, Dakota Territory.

But Johnny had seen Comanches in Texas steal hundreds of horses at a time, and he had thrilled to the adventure of stealing them back. Shortly after he started prospecting on Castle Creek, Indians stole his horse. Johnny remembered why he hated Indians and why he missed the adventure of stealing horses. He was one of the West's most efficient horse thieves. His talent brought him an early death, a death still shrouded in mystery.

After losing his horse to Dakota Indians, Johnny borrowed another and rode alone to the Red Cloud Agency. He shot the Indian guard and stampeded the tribe's 300-horse herd. He single-handedly herded them to the Black Hills. When the horse he rode tired, he would rope another and continue on. He cached his herd on Upper French Creek and gave up prospecting for dealing in horses.

Johnny bragged about stealing horses from Indians, but never admitted stealing from whites. Stealing horses from whites was considered a capital offense, with or without benefit of legal due process. There is also some evidence that Johnny branched out into stage robbing.

One of Johnny's best-known escapades happened in a raid on the Cheyenne Agency. He had two helpers, Jim Brocky and Tony Pastor. They only got about seventy horses, but the enraged Indians in hot pursuit made it all the adventure Johnny wanted.

Brocky was seriously wounded, and the thieves and their stolen herd got lost in a blizzard. Brocky begged Johnny to shoot him. Johnny refused. He tied Brocky to his horse and whipped him with a quirt, hoping to make him mad enough to want to live. When Brocky insisted on the mercy bullet, Johnny laid him down in the blowing snow, tied their best saddle horse nearby, and hoped Brocky would gather enough strength to follow.

Brocky never made it. Johnny and Pastor were nearly frozen when they got thirteen of the horses to shelter in a ravine. Pastor was hanged shortly after, although not for stealing horses from Indians.

In October, 1878, robbers held up a stagecoach near Buffalo Gap Station, about fifty miles south of Rapid City. Someone recognized Johnny as one of the robbers. At that time Frank Smith, a livestock detective from Cheyenne, was in the area looking for Johnny with a warrant for horse theft.

About a week after the stage robbery, Smith arrested Johnny on the Pine Ridge Indian Reservation. With Johnny in his custody, Smith took the stage for Deadwood. He got Boone May to ride escort.

Boone May hated Johnny from their days together as law officers. May had the reputation of shooting prisoners for the fun of it. He always said they were trying to escape and he had to shoot. One time May had learned about a bounty on an outlaw who had already been killed. May dug up the body, cut off the head, and carried it to Cheyenne for his reward. The authorities had denied him the money, saying there was no proof he had killed the outlaw.

As the stage carrying Johnny descended toward a timber-lined creek, the shotgun messenger, Jesse Brown, decided to get off and walk a while. At the same time Boone May rode away toward a nearby freight road, and Frank Smith dropped back out of sight.

The only passengers in the stage other than Johnny when a masked man rode up were the shotgun messenger's wife and daughters. They said the masked man shot Johnny and carried him into the timber toward the freight road. They ran back down the stage road screaming for Brown. He and Frank Smith returned and said they wondered what had happened to Boone May. They reported Johnny's abduction when the stage reached Deadwood.

The next day Pete Oslund, a bullwhacker friend of Johnny's, saw his body hanging from a tree next to the creek where the claimed abduction had occurred. He cut the body down and buried it.

Johnny was popular with many people in the Black Hills. They named the creek where he was killed Lame Johnny Creek, and a lake near present Mount Rushmore Horsethief Lake in his honor.

To add to the mystery, ten years after the hanging two men dug up Johnny's body. The head was missing. Some wondered if Boone May had another skull on his mantle.

Suggested reading: Helen Rezatto, *Tales of the Black Hills* (Rapid City: Fenwyn Press, 1989).

I CAME HERE TO DIE

Crawford Goldsby, born in 1876 in Fort Concho, Texas, was a racial goulash — Black, White, Cherokee, Mexican, and Sioux. Goldsby started early in crime. At fourteen he killed his brother-in-law in an argument over hogs. The worst renegade in the Indian Territory, he killed for the love of killing. The people called him Cherokee Bill.

The outlaw coveted women as much as he loved killing. He had a girl in every section of the territory. His favorite was Maggie Glass.

When the U. S. Marshal's office got its arrest warrant, Deputy Marshal Ike Rogers, Maggie's cousin, set up a meeting between Maggie and Bill. Maggie suspected treachery and warned Bill to leave.

"Let Rogers make his play," Bill laughed. "I'll show him how fast I can do another murder."

Rogers watched for thirty-six hours. Then, at four one morning, Rogers struck Bill's head with a heavy stove poker. Another deputy helped him tie Bill up with baling wire.

Bill was wanted for scores of robberies and three murders at that time. The marshals took him to Fort Smith for trial on the most vicious of the murders. Bill had deliberately shot down an unarmed citizen during one of the robberies.

Isaac Parker, the hanging judge, found Bill guilty and sentenced him to death.

Someone smuggled a six-gun in to Bill, and he shot and killed a guard. Then he tried to break the entire jail open and release all 250 of its inmates. More than a hundred shots were fired by other guards before Bill gave up and surrendered his weapon.

Convicted of the guard's murder, Bill again heard Judge Parker pronounce death by hanging.

"You are undoubtedly the most ferocious monster, and your record more atrocious than all the criminals who have hitherto stood before this bar," Parker said. "It is too bad that courts can go no further than destroy life, and that one execution must serve to mete justice to the multiplex murderer, the same as to those who have only one such crime for which to answer."

On March 17, 1896, Cherokee Bill walked to the gallows in front of six hundred spectators. The hangman strapped Bill's ankles together, and the marshal read the death warrant.

"Do you want to say anything to the crowd," the marshal asked.

"No. I came here to die, not to make a speech."

The trap was released and Bill fell through to his death. He had had his twentieth birthday the month before.

Suggested reading: S. W. Harman, *Hell on the Border* (Fort Smith: Phoenix Publishing Co., 1898).

CHEROKEE BILL

Western History Collections, University of Oklahoma Libraries

A BAD HANGING FOR A BAD MAN

Most men on the scaffold showed little emotion. They may have trembled inside, but their calm behavior masked their fear. A few like Jack Slade became craven cowards, dropping to their knees to beg for life. Tom (Black Jack) Ketchum showed something else.

In October, 1900, Ketchum was sentenced to death in Clayton, New Mexico, for "molesting a train." This would be the first legal execution in that part of the country, and the date was treated as a general holiday for the entertainment of all. On the eve of the event Ketchum was asked for his last wish.

His response — Bring me a woman for the night — shocked the community. The tradition of granting a criminal's last wish was almost sacred, but the men of Clayton were married or had respectable female relatives. How could they face such women if they granted that wish? Besides, if a woman in the community was available, no official would admit knowing who it could be. After hours of futile and very private debate, the officials told Ketchum that no public funds were available for such a purpose.

Ketchum did not take the refusal politely. He told them they could all kiss a hidden part of his body. For that purpose they could bury him face downward and not have to turn him over.

People thronged into Clayton the next morning to see the last of Black Jack Ketchum. A holiday spirit pervaded the town. A special tour from Raton and Trinidad brought leading citizens from those communities. Many of them had seen men hanged, but only in amateur ventures, without legal authority. This hanging was legal and would be done by a professional! They depended on sheriff Salome Garcia to provide the entertainment.

Black Jack had gained weight during his long stay in jail. The sheriff provided too much rope, Black Jack fell too far, and the drop severed his head from his torso. It was one of the worst hangings in the West. One might say it couldn't have happened to a more deserving fellow.

Suggested reading: William French, *Further Recollections of a Western Ranchman* (New York: Argosy-Antiquarian, 1965).

BLACK JACK KETCHUM

Western History Collections, University of Oklahoma Libraries

BORDER TROUBLE

One of the most gruesome but little-known battles in the West happened near El Paso on February 18, 1881. Events started three weeks earlier when a drunk peddler flashed a large roll of bills in a cabaret in Paso del Norte on the Mexican side of the river.

Three American thieves took over. They took the drunk for a walk and helped themselves to what they found in his pocket.

"Let's go get a drink," one of the thieves said.

Back in the saloon, enjoying the fruits of their nighttime expedition, the surprised thieves saw the same drunk still flashing a large roll.

They took him for another walk and found another bundle in a different pocket.   One wonders at their carelessness on the first search.

When the thieves again laughed and lapped it up back at the saloon, the drunk reappeared, still flashing money!

This time, their reputations at stake, the three thieves did it right. They grabbed the drunk under the arms, dragged him outside to the desert, and stripped him completely. A thorough search of every pocket and seam produced more money.   A total of eight hundred dollars in *pesos* had now been transferred from Mexican to American ownership.

The naked victim went straight to the police, who were incensed. They rounded up every American in town, seven all together.

The arrested men were a hard lot, but they had friends in El Paso, principally the Manning brothers, James, Frank, and John.   The brothers stirred El Paso into an uproar over the arrests. Threats to Mexican officials and demands for quick release brought Mexican promises of early trials so the innocent could be released.

When three weeks passed and the cases had not even appeared on the court docket, the talk in El Paso turned to jail break.

Mexican law allowed conjugal visits to men in jail or prison. Wives and girl friends were allowed to visit in private. So on February 18 smiling guards waved several large-breasted girls from El Paso on through for their visits. They didn't notice that the girls appeared more "busty" than usual. Each carried a forty-five, hidden high in her dress.

The Paso del Norte jail was enclosed by an adobe wall,

too high to climb, its single entrance guarded by a squad of soldiers. Frank Thompson was the first American out. He kicked open the gate and shot the guard captain and one soldier. When another soldier rose up to fight, Thompson clubbed him unconscious. Pat Ryan followed Thompson out the gate, but lost his nerve when he reached the first saloon. He took cover behind the bar and waited to surrender. The Lafayette Kid charged out next, stumbled into a ditch, and gave up. Only Frank O'Neal and J. C. Cain joined Thompson in a real attempt at escape. These three were probably the thieves who started it all.

Thompson, O'Neal, and Cain ran north toward the river. A nameless *vaquero* was eating in a restaurant when he heard the shooting. He mounted his horse, drew his rifle from the scabbard, and rode in pursuit. He caught up with the three as they were crossing a deep irrigation ditch.

The escapers opened fire on their mounted pursuer. But they were in chest-high water, their aim poor, their pistols short-ranged. The *vaquero's* rifle sounded three times, and all three men sank to death in a watery grave.

Mexicans recovered the bodies and tied them to tails of burros for a victory parade through the center of Paso del Norte. Watchers, many of them from the criminal element of El Paso, viewed the ghastly procession from high vantage points. Lifeless arms and legs flapped hideously as the three-part carrion jolted through the streets and over sharp rocks. Friends (and former colleagues) of the victims swore vengeance.

Law abiding residents of El Paso, also infuriated at the international insult, tried to recover the bodies from the Mexican officials. The demand rose to seventy-five dollars per corpse, too high a price. The cadavers were rolled into a ditch and covered with dirt.

Three months later the last of the remaining prisoners (apparently all innocent men) escaped from the jail, this time successfully.

Justice had finally triumphed!

Suggested reading: Leon C. Metz, *Dallas Stoudenmire, El Paso Marshal* (Norman: Univ. of Okla. Press, 1979).

THINNING OUT THE BAD MEN

John Wesley Hardin was the most cold-blooded killer in the West. His father, a Methodist minister, named the boy after the founder of his faith, not knowing he'd become so interested in cards and gunplay.

By the time he was sixteen, Hardin thought nothing of sitting down to a poker game with $350 in gold. Once he dealt full houses to three players and four jacks to himself.

Hardin killed his first man in 1868. Within a month he had killed three more. In 1871 he followed a cattle herd up the Chisholm Trail, killing six men on the trail and three more when they reached Abilene. The eighteen-year-old now had thirteen notches in his pistol.

Hardin, a small man, was brim full of meanness. He enjoyed killing impudent negroes, Yankee soldiers, and carpetbaggers in post-Civil War Texas. Soon he branched out to kill any and all who got in his way.

Hardin had an over-grown ego. He bragged that most of his victims were shot squarely between the eyes. Once when he was riding the Chisholm Trail some Indians stopped the trail crew, demanding the usual beef to butcher and eat. When Hardin refused, an Indian drew his pistol, saying if the cowboys did not give him a steer he would kill one himself. Hardin replied that if the Indian killed a steer, Hardin would kill him. "Well he killed the beef, and I killed him," Hardin wrote. Hardin said he "mounted" the dead steer by tying the dead Indian to its back.

When three deputy sheriffs chased Hardin out of Abilene, he rode for thirty-five miles before stopping to get the drop on his pursuers. Then he disarmed them, took all their clothing and boots, and chased their horses away. The men walked back to Abilene in sweltering July weather.

In 1878 Hardin was sentenced to twenty-five years for killing a deputy sheriff. He served sixteen and was pardoned. While in prison he read law and theology and served as superintendent of the prison Sunday School. He was admitted to practice law upon his release.

After visiting his children at his Gonzales home — his wife had died while he was in prison — he had a short, unsuccessful marriage with a young girl and then moved to El Paso to assist in the prosecution of a criminal case. The citizens welcomed him as a leading member of the bar! There he took up with Beulah, the wife of Martin M'Rose, a friend of his. M'Rose, who rode with a long rope and a watchful eye for stray steers, had married the voluptuous blonde in a whorehouse. Shortly after Beulah's new liaison, her husband was killed by George Scarborough and two other officers. Beulah loved the bright lights and the bottle. While Hardin was out of town she put on a wild West exhibition that got her arrested by a young El Paso policeman, John Selman. Selman's father, a nondescript gunman, had recently served as an El Paso constable. Hardin, returning home, was furious about Beulah's arrest. He told Old John Selman that his son was a coward.

It would be hard to find a man more callous than John Wesley Hardin. But on August 19, 1895, as Hardin was shaking dice in the Acme saloon in El Paso, just such a man walked in. Old John Selman had killed over twenty men in his life, including the part spent as a peace officer.

Hardin, who had killed forty-three, was standing with his back to the front entrance when Selman entered. He had just called out, "Four sixes to beat," when Selman drew his pistol, put it against the back of Hardin's head and fired. Hardin dropped dead in his tracks.

Selman justified his actions by saying Hardin could have seen him by looking in the mirror behind the bar. But he also said he shot Hardin in the eye and the bullet came out at the back of the head.

The doctor called to testify at the coroner's inquest said, "If he shot him in the eye, it was excellent marksmanship. If in the back of the head, it was excellent judgment."

El Paso newspapers commented that the bad men were benefitting the community by thinning out their own ranks.

George Scarborough was charged with killing M'Rose in what appeared to be a friendly prosecution to put the stamp of approval on that killing. Before his trial and before Selman came to trial for killing Hardin, Scarborough and Selman were walking down the street together. Selman tried to shoot Scarborough, but Scarborough's six-gun response transferred Selman's problems to a higher court and eliminated the need to prosecute him in El Paso.

We don't know what happened to Beulah.

Suggested reading: John Wesley Hardin, *Life of John Wesley Hardin As Written by Himself* (Norman: Univ. of Okla. Press, 1961).

ORDEAL IN THE CANYON

In mid-June, 1897, Dr. George Medar and Captain Richard Thomas put their specially-built boat into the Colorado River at Lee's Ferry, Arizona. The men, both scientists, would float to the river's mouth, gathering information and mapping the route. They soon saw what appeared to be four stranded boatmen along the narrow shore in a deep canyon. They turned in to see if they could help.

The men were outlaws, two of them just escaped from jail in Utah. The leader, Jim LaRoche, met the scientists with drawn guns, thinking they were part of the posse chasing them. Joe Harris, Alfredo Farias, and Victorio Mescalero, stood behind Harris as the astonished scientists pulled to shore.

"Now isn't this just dandy," Harris said. "We can float clear to Yuma and the posse'll never see us."

They grabbed Medar and Thomas, bound them hand and foot, and threw them back into the boat. Then LaRoche went into a cove and returned with two Navajo girls they had captured earlier that morning — Ramona Uuyot, sixteen, and her fourteen-year-old sister, Conchita.

Before starting downstream LaRoche discovered the two gallons of whiskey the scientists had laid in for their two-month journey. The outlaws were soon drunk. Thomas protested that the boat could not carry eight passengers over the rapids ahead.

"You're right," LaRoche said. "We got too many." He drew his revolver and shot Thomas in the chest. "Throw him over the side, Vic."

The terrified girls cowered in the prow as Thomas' body rolled in the current and disappeared. The LaRoche turned his gun toward Dr. Medar. Harris restrained him.

"One shot was enough," Harris said. "We don't want that posse to know where we are."

So they took Medar's money, his watch, and his diamond ring. Then, as he begged for his life, they threw him, still bound, into the roiling water.

At their camp that evening, Mescalero began molesting Ramona.

"Stay away from her," LaRoche growled," she's mine."

Mescalero, drunk again, threw a rock at LaRoche and let out a war whoop.

"Cut that out," Harris ordered. "You want that posse down on us?" He turned to LaRoche. "You should know better than to give an Indian whisky."

LaRoche and Harris matched coins for the girls. Harris won and chose Ramona. But tensions among the four outlaws were building. Ramona had found Dr. Medar's diary and began making surreptitious entries.

Rough water and rapids the next day left them soaked when they stopped to camp. As they ate supper, one of the bound bodies floated past. The men played poker until after midnight, Farias the big winner.

"I'll put all my winnings up against your Conchita," he told LaRoche.

LaRoche agreed. Farias won with a pair. He chucked the girl under the chin. "You're mine now, baby. Won fair and square. I'll go get our blankets."

Farias headed for the boat, LaRoche stalking behind.

Scuffling sounds came from the river, and LaRoche returned alone. He grabbed Conchita and headed into the brush.

"Where's Al?" Harris asked.

"Went for a walk."

They shoved off the next morning in a rain. No one spoke of the blood stained rocks at the river's edge, but everyone knew that LaRoche had knifed Farias and pushed him into the river.

With only five passengers, the boat rode higher in the water, but they barely survived the next day's rapids and twisting currents. During the roughest water, Mescalero rigged a rope from the boat to a tree and served as anchorman, playing the rope out as the boat shot the rapids. When they pulled him in he was unconscious, a deep cut in his head from a jagged rock. Earlier that day they saw the body of Farias, where it had washed ashore.

Ramona found a medicine kit and treated Mescalero's wound. By the time they found a landing place, the Indian was conscious but very weak.

In the meantime the posse had found the outlaws' horses, had learned about the scientists, and knew that the Indian girls were missing. The deputy sheriff in charge decided to station men at places where landing spots had access to the canyon rim.

But LaRoche decided on a bold move. They had plenty of food. Why not release the boat and hide out until the posse, seeing the empty boat, had decided that they had all drowned? Harris agreed.

Ramona wrote on July 22: The men are very careful.

They know we are being watched.

The next day Conchita was very sick. The girls could hear voices on the rim above them. They stayed in camp until LaRoche and Harris had built a raft. Mescalero's condition had worsened by the time they shoved the raft into the river. Conchita also showed no improvement.

Conchita died on September 4. Two days later Mescalero gave Ramona his share of the money stolen from the scientists and Farias. He told her to hide it in her dress. He died that night.

Both bodies were covered with rocks, so circling buzzards would not disclose their location. Four days before, the posse had given up, concluding that the outlaws and the Indian girls had perished.

The raft had to be abandoned when it would no longer carry the three passengers and their supplies. Harris moved downstream, climbing over rocks. He reached a point where he thought they could get to the canyon rim. He tied a rope around his waist and started climbing. Whenever he reached a ledge, he used the rope to pull LaRoche and Ramona up to him. But suddenly a rock gave way, and Harris plunged into the canyon, screaming hysterically.

"I should have got his money, first," LaRoche grumbled.

Ramona was a thousand feet below the rim with a man she had come to despise. But Harris' accident had made LaRoche more cautious. He climbed carefully, pulling Ramona up with the rope as Harris had done. Late that night they finally stood on flat ground. Ramona was too tired to know how they had done it. They slept in the brush, huddled together to stay warm.

Ramona had kept the diary and the money from Mescalero hidden in her dress. LaRoche told her to stay under cover while he looked for horses. Shortly after he left, she fled into the brush. Several hours later she was picked up and taken to the sheriff, where she told her amazing story.

A posse found LaRoche's trail and then lost it. They found the bodies of the scientists and Conchita.

About a year later, LaRoche tried to contact Ramona. She told the sheriff he was in the area. When the posse found him, he came out shooting. One shot brought him down. Before he died, he confessed to five murders. He asked that his money be given to Ramona.

Suggested reading: Tom Bailey, "Murder Rode the Colorado," in *Frontier Times* v. 35, no. 4, Fall, 1961).

LAST STAGECOACH BANDIT

The last person to rob a western stage was the only woman to commit that crime. Her name was Pearl Hart.

Pearl Taylor grew up in a respectable family in Lindsay, Ontario, Canada. She left her finishing school at seventeen to elope with Frederick Hart. Life with the small-time gambler and part-time bartender was touch and go. In 1893 Fred worked as barker for sideshows at the Columbian Exposition in Chicago. Pearl had odd jobs and enough time on her hands to see the Buffalo Bill Wild West show. She went to most of the performances, and consorted with the participants. She fell in love with the Old West, believing everything she saw in the arena and everything the actors told her in private.

Pearl left Fred and stopped in Colorado long enough to bear a son. After leaving the baby with her mother in Ontario, Pearl returned west, this time to Arizona.

She soon learned that the Old West was not like Buffalo Bill had portrayed it in Chicago. She got by with laundry and cooking jobs until Fred showed up in 1895. He promised to get work if Pearl took him back. She didn't think she had any choice.

Three more years of bartending brought some domestic happiness and another baby, a girl. But Fred beat Pearl up and joined Roosevelt's Rough Riders to fight in Cuba. Pearl parked the baby with its older brother and returned to western mining camps.

She continued cooking and took up with Joe Boot, a miner. In 1899 Pearl learned that her mother was ill and needed money for Pearl's children.

Boot, not known for brains, suggested they hold up the stage that ran from Florence, Arizona, to Globe.

"I thought they stopped robbing stages," Pearl said. "Trains carry all the money now."

"That's just the point. They don't have shotgun messengers any more. Most drivers don't even carry guns."

"Then why hold it up?"

"They always got salesmen on board. They must carry money. The Globe stage is one of the last in the country. Should be a pushover."

They waited at a watering hole where the drivers always stopped. Pearl had an old .44 Colt. Joe carried a newer .45.

They jumped out in front of the stage as it approached. The driver thought Pearl, dressed in man's clothing, was a boy. He handed her his gun. While Joe held the horses and watched the driver, Pearl collected $450 from the three passengers.

"See, just like I said," Joe reminded her.

Then Pearl, remembering some scene from Cody's show, gallantly peeled off three ones. "For grub and a place to spend the night," she said, handing the bills back.

They ordered the driver to go on, mounted their horses, and rode away. But they had already used up all the thought they had put into planning. They promptly got lost.

After wandering for several days, they fell asleep one night at their brightly blazing campfire. The posse woke them up.

Pearl played her role with everything she had.

"You never would've taken me alive if I'd gotten to my gun," she told the smiling lawmen.

An overnight celebrity, she strutted in her cell and tried to play the part of a serious outlaw. But a few days later, she and another prisoner — not Joe Boot — escaped.

News of the manhunt added to her growing legend. Soon captured, she again played the part of a desperado. She even made a flamboyant suicide attempt.   "I don't want to live in this jail another day," she said to the guard as she tossed a white powder into her mouth and suddenly collapsed.

A doctor rushed to her aid and made his examination. Then he said, "Oh stop it, Pearl. Get on your feet."

She opened one eye and peeked.

"You can't kill yourself with talcum powder."

Pearl insisted that no court had the right to try her for a crime. The overlooked champion of womens' liberation said indignantly, "I can't be tried under a law which my sex had nothing to do with making."

Tried separately from Boot, the jury acquitted her.

The furious judge ordered another jury empaneled immediately to try her again, this time for stealing the gun from the driver. He instructed the jury plainly about letting sympathy for a woman cloud their reason. This jury found her guilty in ten minutes. The judge gave her five years.

Suggested reading: Jay Nash, *Encyclopedia of Western Lawmen and Outlaws* (New York: Da Capo Press, 1994).

PEARL HART

Arizona Historical Society, Tucson   AHS 28916

WE'LL OUTDO THE OTHER GANGS

"We'll beat Jesse and the Youngers," vowed Bob Dalton. "We'll stick up two banks at the same damned time — in broad daylight."

The Indian Territory outlaw was talking about his relatives. The Younger brothers were first cousins; the James Brothers more distantly related.

Earier, Bob Dalton had served briefly as a deputy U. S. Marshal out of Fort Smith. Then he and brothers Grat, also a one-time marshal at Fort Smith, and Emmet turned to bank robbery. In February, 1891, to escape lawmen in Indian Territory and Kansas, they moved to California for their first train robbery. Their holdup of a Southern Pacific passenger train near Tulare (at present Earlimart, California), produced a dead fireman, little loot, and the most unbelievable escape in the history of the West.

The disappointed train robbers had holed up with their brother Bill, who lived nearby. But the posse found Grat, and the judge sentenced him to twenty years in Folsom prison.

Two armed deputies guarded Grat as their train headed north from Fresno. They knew he was an athlete and totally fearless, so they kept his feet tied together and one of his arms manacled to one of the deputies at all times. Besides, it was a day train, full of passengers, so escape on the way to prison seemed impossible.

The train was going at full speed — forty-five miles an hour — when it came alongside the swift-running San Joaquin River. The unmanacled deputy dozed in the April heat. Suddenly the other deputy was astonished to see Grat leap to his feet, the handcuff falling away. Before the deputy could draw his gun, Grat dove head first out a window. The screaming passengers on that side saw him plunge into the river and disappear.

The deputies stopped the train and rushed down to the river. All they found was the leather thong that had tied their prisoner and fresh hoof prints from two horses. Grat and Emmet were soon back in Indian Territory.

After three more train robberies and four murders, Bob made his vow to outshine the Younger and James gangs. By now the Daltons had added Bill Powers and Dick Broadwell to their gang. They picked Coffeyville, Kansas, for their raid. The Daltons had grown up there and knew the streets and alleys well. The two banks in town were practically side by side.

Mounted on good Thoroughbred horses, the five men rode into Coffeyville from the west about nine-thirty the morning of Wednesday, October 5, 1892. They turned down Maple Street to the alley between Eighth and Ninth, dismounted, and tied their horses to a fence at the rear of the city jail. They continued east in the alley, passing several people, none of whom seemed alarmed at five heavily armed men walking toward the town plaza and its two banks.

When the alley opened in to the plaza, the robbers broke into a dog trot, their rifles ready. Grat, Powers, and Broadwell entered the Condon bank in the center of the plaza, while Bob and Emmet crossed a vacant lot and hurried into the First National. By now, the people could see what was happening. "The Daltons are robbing the banks," they called out.

Inside the Condon bank, Grat demanded that all the bank's money be put into a two-bushel sack which he produced.

"The time lock doesn't go off until 9:45," said the quick-thinking cashier.

Grat looked at his watch, not noticing that the safe was already open. "Just three minutes," he said. "We'll wait."

In the meantime, Bob and Emmet ordered the First National cashier to hand over all the money in that bank. The cashier, Tom Ayers, took his time bringing the currency and

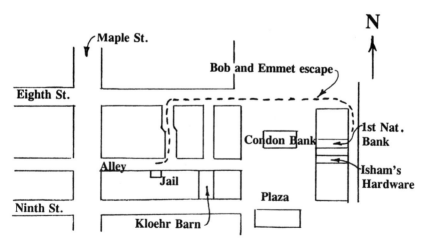

gold to the counter. When the robbers had their grain sack filled, they tried to leave by the front door. A heavy fusillade of lead swept across the plaza, and changed their minds. Now they would have to go out the back door, run down the alley to Eighth Street, and hope they could reach their horses.

But too many Coffeyville citizens had now joined the battle. When Lucius Baldwin, a store clerk, heard the alarm, he ran into Isham's Hardware, two doors from the First National, to get a pistol. Then he ran out the back door, hoping to take the robbers in the rear. One of the Daltons shot him through the heart, and Baldwin died on the spot.

Bob and Emmet ran down the alley to Eighth Street and turned west, trying to get back to their horses. When they reached the plaza, they saw many men pouring lead into the Condon bank. They also saw George Cubine, pistol in hand, watching the front door of the First National. Beside him stood Charles Brown, a harmless old man, unarmed. Cubine had been a good friend of the Dalton brothers. Bob, who so far had not been seen, could not resist stopping and shooting his old friend in the back. As Cubine fell to the ground, Brown picked up the pistol from his companion's dead hand. Bob fired again and Brown fell, one dead body on top of another.

When the Daltons went out the bank's back door, cashier Tom Ayers ran out the front to Isham's hardware, where he got a rifle. When he heard the gunfire of Bob shooting Cubine and Brown, he looked out the hardware store window and saw the Daltons. Ayers knelt so he could aim carefully at his target, seventy yards away. All Bob Dalton could see was Ayers' head as he fired. Ayers slumped to the floor, shot through the head. Bob and Emmet laughed and ran on west, finally reaching their horses. At this point the score was four to nothing in favor of the bandits over the town defenders.

Back in the Condon bank, the three robbers waited stubbornly for the three minutes to pass. It seemed like the whole town was firing through the bank's windows at them. When they heard Bob Dalton's first rifle shot behind them, they decided it was time to leave. They would have to settle for what money they had and forget about the safe, which, unknown to them, had been open all the time. They dashed across the plaza and down the alley toward their horses.

A whole squad of men in front of Isham's Hardware, with a clear view down the alley, were pouring out a withering fire. Marshal Charles Connelly, with a rifle borrowed from Swisher's gun shop, ran into the alley to the west of the robbers, unaware that they were behind him. Grat, though wounded himself, killed the marshal with a bullet in the back. The score now stood five to zero. Grat, Powers and Broadwell all wounded, reached the horses, just after Bob and Emmet got there.

Bob had tied his sack containing $20,000 to his saddle horn. "We've got the swag," he shouted. "Let's get out of here."

Then John Kloehr, who ran a livery barn and was the town's best shot, entered the action. He had borrowed a rifle from Barndollar's general store, ran through his barn, and took up a position not fifty feet from where the robbers had reached their horses.

Just after Bob Dalton killed the marshal, Kloehr dropped him dead. Grat saw Kloehr's shot and lifted his rifle to fire. But Kloehr's Winchester spoke first, and Grat fell dead, a hole exactly in the center of his throat.

Powers tried to mount his horse but someone in the squad on Isham's porch got him in the chest and he fell dead. The score was evening up fast.

Broadwell and Emmet got into their saddles, and they raced down the alley. A new volley made Broadwell reel and sent blood spurting from his mouth, but he spurred his horse and kept going. Then Emmet, at twenty the youngest of the brothers, did an incredible thing.

Emmet reined his horse in, turned around and rode back up the alley, straight into the blistering fire from the defenders of Coffeyville. He reined up where Bob lay dead, dismounted, and tried to lift his brother into the saddle that he might bear him away.

A rifle bullet shattered his arm, and Bob's body slipped away. Emmet tried again, but a load of buckshot hit him in the side and back. Then more shots shattered his arm, broke his leg, and he fell, unconscious.

Broadwell rode on, bleeding from a dozen wounds. The victorious citizens found him a mile away, dead at the roadside. The score would end, five to four. The whole war had lasted less than fifteen minutes.

Emmet recovered, was sent to prison, and got pardoned after fourteen years. He went into the California real estate business and wrote a book about himself and his brothers which became a movie. He died at sixty-five.

Suggested reading: An Eye Witness (probably Edgar Vermont, Coffeyville reporter) *The Dalton Brothers* (New York: Frederick . Fell, Inc., 1954).

HE DIED LIKE A PITIABLE CHICKEN THIEF

Unlike some of his brothers, Bill Dalton started out as a law abiding man. He moved to Merced County, California, in the early 1880s. He took up farming and married the daughter of a wealthy farmer. He entered politics under the tutelage of the Merced County district attorney. A smart man and well-read, Bill Dalton was soon elected to the California legislature.

But in 1891 brothers Bob, Grat, and Emmett came to California and held up a Southern Pacific Train. Bill apparently had nothing to do with the robbery, but he was arrested as a conspirator anyway. The jury found him not guilty, but Bill held a grudge. He probably assisted Grat as the convicted brother made his fantastic escape.

Bill was back in Kingfisher, Oklahoma, visiting his mother at the time of the great Coffeyville shootout, where the nine dead included brothers Bob and Grat.

After Bill Doolin reorganized the survivors of the Dalton gang, Bill Dalton became his first recruit. Dalton's grudge had now grown to a furious demand for revenge on society.

After the invasion of Ingalls in which Bill Dalton took an important part, the gang split up in early 1894 and scattered until the heat went down. Then on May 23 Dalton and three other bandits rode into Longview, Texas, and held up the First National Bank.

One of the men presented this note to the cashier:

The First National Bank, Longview:
This will introduce to you Charles Speckelmeyer, who wants some money and is going to have it.
B and F

The cashier, thinking the note was asking for a charitable subscription, started to donate. Then the robber pulled a rifle from under his slicker and announced that it was a holdup. One outlaw, Jim Wallace, was killed in the fight.

On June 4 two men bought a wagon in the Chickasaw Nation of Indian Territory with bills taken in the Longview robbery. Three days later Houston Wallace, a dirt-poor farmer who lived twenty-five miles from Ardmore, drove into town with his wife and a pretty blonde stranger. Wallace paid cash for ammunition and a large stock of groceries.

Officers suspected they had located the hideout of the

Longview bandits, and a posse soon formed.

The next day, as the posse surrounded the Wallace house, they saw a man come to the door and look out. He ducked back inside, grabbed a revolver, and jumped from a window, running for a ravine. Deputy Marshal Loss Hart dropped him with one shot. When Hart reached the dying man demanding to know his name, the man smiled inscrutably as though happy he had not been recognized.

The officers found only six frightened children inside the house. Two of the smallest admitted that their name was Dalton.

The officers loaded the corpse in a wagon and started for Ardmore. On the way they met a wagon containing the two women they had talked to before. Deputy S. T. Lindsay spoke to the pretty blonde:

"Mrs. Dalton, we have your husband and on his person we found considerable money . . ."

"I am not Mrs. Dalton and you have not got Bill."

But when the wagon pulled up and she looked at the dead body, she broke down completely. Hysterically she admitted that the dead man was Bill and she was his wife.

Jennie Dalton took her husband's body back to Merced, California, and had it buried there.

And old fisherman near Longview, with whom the gang had spent the day before the robbery, identified Dalton from a peculiar patch on the instep of his boot. The bank cashier also identified him as the man who had presented the introductory note.

Colonel Clarence Douglas, Ardmore resident and correspondent for the *Daily Oklahoman,* closed his report about the Longview robbery:

It has often been said that when Bill Dalton died he would go to the shadowy land accompanied by a number of his pursuers, and that any man that faced him in the last great duel of his life would bear him company. But he was killed like some pitiable chicken thief, and the glamour of romance and daring thrown around his life by his brave and lawless deeds before the facts of his death prove once more that law and justice are supreme and must in the end be triumphant.

Suggested reading: Glenn Shirley, *Six-gun and Silver Star* (Albuquerque: Univ. of New Mexico Press, 1955).

ROSE OF THE CIMARRON

Rose Dunn's parents made the Oklahoma land rush in 1889, settling on a quarter-section east of what would become the town of Ingalls. The family, on both sides, had handsome men and beautiful women. Slim and dark, Rose's blue-black hair and clear, golden complexion gave her a gypsy-like beauty. Her family had more money and education than most, and Rose went to a convent at thirteen to be educated. Her beauty and poise made her stand out among her country girl neighbors.

But Rose was a true daughter of the frontier. She helped her mother tend the chickens and the garden. While she had better clothing than her neighbors, her sewing machine-made dresses came from tattered patterns passed along by the town ladies. She grew up a skilled rider and an expert shot with pistol and Winchester.

Ingalls became the headquarters of the Doolin gang, led by Bill Doolin, one of America's last famous outlaws. After the citizens of Coffeyville, Kansas, had put an end to the Dalton gang, Bill Doolin reorganized the survivors. Doolin had been a cowboy on the HX Bar Ranch on the Cimarron River. But the land rush put cowboys out of work, and Doolin turned to crime. His gang robbed trains and banks and stole horses in Indian Territory and Texas.

George "Bitter Creek" Newcomb had been one of Doolin's closest friends ever since they worked together on the HX Bar. Newcomb became one of the first to join the new robber band.

Both Newcomb and Doolin were devil-may-care riders who loved adventure, liquor, and poker. Tall and slender, expert with wild broncs, lariats, and six-guns, they attracted frontier girls. By 1893 the gang had become one of the most deadly groups of outlaws in Western history. Unlike Jesse James, they never whined or made excuses. They wanted to be outlaws, and they enjoyed the work.

Rose Dunn's social life revolved around church box suppers in Ingalls, dances at Pawnee, and singing around the organ at home. But her brothers did a little rustling from time to time, and she knew how to help. She fell in love with Bitter Creek Newcomb.

Rose began to ride with her lover's gang. Frontier outlaws could shoot down helpless bank employees and steal another man's cattle and horses, but they never forced their attentions on a woman who belonged to another gang member. All treated her with respect. Not even in Ingalls was there a word of gossip against her.

In late July, 1893, a red-headed stranger showed up in Ingalls. He said his name was Red Lucas, just passing through. He was a good poker player and the gang liked him, so he stayed a month. Rose told Bitter Creek that she was uneasy about Lucas.

"Let's ride to Texas," she pleaded. "A change of scenery will do us good."

He laughed away her fears.

But on September 1, about thirty United States marshals and deputies, disguised as a ranch outfit, camped outside Ingalls. Their carefully made plans for attacking the town resulted from information provided by Lucas. They divided to attack from three directions at once.

Rose, talking to Mrs. Pierce at the Pierce hotel, saw a boy run up, warning that the marshals were coming. She took the terrified boy to Trilby's, where the gang was playing poker. They didn't believe the boy. Newcomb calmed Rose's fears and she returned to the hotel.

With rifles loaded and wagons carrying supplies, the marshals moved in silently, one group toward the Hotel, one to Trilby's, and one to the livery barn.

After a time, Newcomb felt restless. He threw down his hand and stood up.

"Where yuh goin', kid?" Doolin asked.

"Think I'll ride down to the pump and look around."

The game resumed.

Revolvers and rifles trained stealthily on Newcomb as he rode down the street. When he reached the hotel he whistled for Rose. She came to the window. He waved at her and rode on.

Suddenly Newcomb pulled up short. He saw Marshal Steve Burke talking to a boy, probably telling him to get out of the line of fire. Bitter Creek and the marshal drew together. Newcomb's hat flew off his head. His bullet tore through Burke's coat. Then the town erupted with gunfire like an artillery barrage rolling in front of advancing infantry. Newcomb spun his horse around and made it back to Trilby's without being hit.

The scene inside Trilby's has been copied in thousands of western movies. The men pushed tables to cover doors and windows. Doolin ran from window to window, firing and encouraging his men. Bullets riddled the wooden walls of the building. Innocent men were caught in the crossfire and gunned down.

One gang member, Arkansas Tom, had been recovering from sickness in his room in the hotel. He killed three marshals from his window while Rose and Mrs. Pierce crouched down in Rose's room. Then Doolin, realizing that their ammunition was running low, ordered his men to make a run for their horses at the livery barn.

The gunfire directed at the hotel let up as the marshals concentrated on the fleeing gang, giving Rose a chance to peek out her window. She saw her lover spilled in the dust, his revolver in his hand but the chambers empty. She grabbed a Winchester, two holstered revolvers, and a bandolier of cartridges, and ran down the hall.

"Rose, what are you doing?" yelled Mrs. Pierce.

"Bitter Creek is wounded. I'm gonna help him."

"Good God, child, you'll be killed out there."

Rose tore strips from a sheet to make a rope, and lowered her armament to the ground. Tying the makeshift rope to a bed post, she slid down and ran with the weapons and cartridges to Bitter Creek. Rose may have counted on western chivalry to help. At any rate, as she ran toward Newcomb, the rifle and bandolier under one arm and the revolvers bouncing against her legs, the gunfire did let up.

When she reached Newcomb, he took the revolvers and continued shooting. Rose knelt at his side, calmly firing the rifle. The marshals' fire resumed.

Doolin shouted above the din of battle: "Hold them off until Rose and the kid get to the barn."

Newcomb was bleeding badly. Rose got him to his feet, buckled his guns around her own slender waist, and half carried, half dragged him to the barn. Doolin and his men helped by laying down a withering fire to keep the marshals at bay.

When the Battle of Ingalls ended, three marshals and four townspeople lay dead, with many more wounded, but all the gang except the sick man in the hotel had escaped. Rose did not go with them. She returned to the bullet-scarred hotel and waited for news.

After dark, Bill Dalton, one of the gang, slipped back into town to tell Rose that Newcomb was still unconscious and needed a doctor badly. Rose got the doctor and rode with him and Dalton to the gang's hideout in the hills. She nursed her lover back to health. As she rode for medicines and food, she kept Doolin posted on the movements of the posses searching for the gang. After several weeks, Newcomb was able to ride. He and Rose moved away to hide out by themselves.

In May, 1894, Newcomb rode with the gang as they robbed a bank in Southwest City, Missouri. Then they were quiet for several months. Newcomb told Rose that he would give up the outlaw trail after a few more strikes. Perhaps they would go to Argentina, a haven at that time for American outlaws wanting to start a new life.

In May, 1895, after a train robbery in Dover, Oklahoma, Doolin called the gang together and said he was through. But it was too late for Rose and Bitter Creek. Marshals and deputies and man hunters looking for rewards searched everywhere. The couple got their sleep in barns and in the open, listening to wolves prowling the hills. Up at dawn, they would spend another day in the saddle, dodging the relentless searchers of Oklahoma.

Then, in early 1896, the saga turned into a Greek tragedy. Rustling charges against Rose's brothers had been dismissed. In return the brothers became deputy marshals and agreed to help find the surviving members of the Doolin gang.

Bitter Creek and Charley Pierce, bone-weary, hungry, and tired of close pursuit by Marshals Bill Tilghman and Heck Thomas, rode up to what they thought was their last refuge, the Dunn Ranch where Rose's brothers lived. They reached the ranch gate and were met by shotgun blasts. The Dunn brothers looked down at their sister's lover and his gang partner, both dead before they slipped to the ground, and put their shotguns away. Some say the brothers did not act solely out of gratitude for getting the charges dismissed, but were trying to protect Rose from Bitter Creek.

In December 1897, nineteen-year-old Rose married Charles Noble, a Lawton blacksmith. After Bitter Creek was shot to death, Noble notified the marshals that Bill Doolin's wife had brought their team into his shop to be shod. This information led to the capture and killing of Bitter Creek's close friend and crime partner, Bill Doolin. The Greek tragedy was complete.

Suggested reading: James D. Horan, *Desperate Women* (New York: G. P. Putnam's Son's, 1952).

THE PLEASURES OF TRAIN ROBBING

Al Jennings, 32-year-old lawyer in an Oklahoma frontier town during the mid-1890s, decided to take down his shingle and become an outlaw. One of the most inept outlaws in the West, he is probably better known for his friendship with a famous writer.

Jennings, a vainglorious braggart full of desperado talk, played the role of a bold and dashing hero, deadly with a gun. While he was county attorney at El Reno, he had met Little Dick West, who had ridden with the Doolin Gang. How the little lawyer, short of stature but long on ego, preened in the reflected light of a real bandit!

Jennings' stupid decision to change careers was made from vengeance. When Temple Houston killed Jennings' brother in a saloon brawl, Al swore to get even. But when Al's friends told him that Temple — son of Texas' Sam Houston — was a skilled gunman and that Al's brother had drawn first, Al backed off. Temple, one of the Southwest's most flamboyant and successful lawyers, represented himself and got an acquittal.

Al Jennings teamed up with another brother, Frank, and started hanging out with Little Dick West and other Oklahoma outlaws. Their first victim was the Santa Fe Railroad on August 16, 1897. They got the drop on the engineer and fireman at a water stop, ordering them to pull the train a mile out of town. They smashed their way into the express car, but couldn't get the safe open. They forgot to rob the passengers.

Next, near Muskogee, they stacked a pile of cross-ties on the tracks to stop a Missouri, Kansas, & Texas train. They watched in disbelief as the engineer charged on through, ties flying in every direction.

Then they tried the Santa Fe near Purcell. Thinking they saw a posse in the distance, they fled. They were lucky. The posse was on the train, waiting for them. Someone had tipped off the railroad.

They shifted to a bank at Minco. Again a posse waited and they were scared off. Their next attempt, a Wells Fargo express car at Berwyn (now called Gene Autry after its singing telegraph agent) produced a little, but not much.

Apparently there was enough to finance a vacation for Al and Frank to the Honduras. There Al became friends with an American, William Sidney Porter, who was waiting trial on

61

an embezzlement charge back in Austin, Texas. They enjoyed drinking together and swapping stories. Al returned in fall 1897 and reunited the gang. They stormed an express car on the Rock Island on October 1. Remembering their first venture when they could not open the safe, they had four sticks of dynamite with them this time. They lit the first stick and ran. The explosion splintered the express car, blew up the remaining dynamite, but did nothing to the safe. Little Dick West decided he was with a bunch of losers and rode away.

Later, in his autobiography, Al emphasized that he was a lawyer turned train robber. "As a lawyer," he wrote, "I was accustomed to look at any proposition from every side. I could not only plan a robbery, but I could prepare get-aways and alibis — provide for any contingency." He could do it, all right, but not very well.

Then one of Al's trusted gang members sold him out. He got life in the Ohio State Prison at Columbus. In those days federal prisoners often served their sentences in state prisons that had room.

In Columbus, Al was reunited with his Honduras friend, who had also been sentenced in his trial in Austin. By then Porter wrote stories under the name, O Henry. He and Al formed a club of trustees for social activities on Sunday afternoons.

Al pulled strings with an Ohio senator and got an early release, only to find himself in Leavenworth to serve out a sentence for shooting a federal marshal. Lawyer Al had foolishly thought he was serving both sentences when he went to Columbus.

He kept in touch with Porter, still serving his sentence. They collaborated on a story entitled, "Holding Up a Train." It was published in *Everybody's Magazine.* Porter wrote this in his preface:

"The man who told me these things was for several years an outlaw in the Southwest. His description of the modus operandi should prove interesting, his counsel of value to the potential passenger in some future "hold-up," while his estimate of the pleasures of train robbing will hardly induce anyone to adopt it as a profession."

Right on, Mister Porter!

Suggested reading: Richard Patterson, *Train Robbery* (Boulder: Johnson Publishing Company, 1981).

ORDERING INFORMATION

True Tales of the Old West is projected for 36 volumes.

Proposed titles include:

Warriors and Chiefs	In print
Soldiers	In print
Native Women	In print
Mountain Men	In print
Pioneer Women	In print
Ranchers and Cowboys	In print
Horses and Riders	In print
Miners	In print
Entertainers	In print
Dogs and Masters	In print
Outlaws	In print
Frontiersmen	In print
Lawmen	Soon to appear
Gamblers	Soon to appear
Homesteaders	Soon to appear
Explorers	Under way
Lawyers & Judges	Under way
Scouts	Under way
Writers	Under way
Railroaders	Started
Merchants	Started
Army Women	Started
Vigilantes	Started

Ask at your bookstore or write:

PIONEER PRESS
Box 216
Carson City, NV 89702-0216